MW01616315

The Songs
We Sing

*A 33,000 Mile Celebration of Threshold Singers,
Community Singing Circles,
and Natural Wonders*

By Susie Joyce

*Lovely Lynda,
Such a joy to
share the love of
song with
you!
Susie*

PARK PLACE PUBLICATIONS
Pacific Grove, California

Published by
Park Place Publications
Pacific Grove, California
www.parkplacepublications.com

ISBN: 978-1-953120-59-5
Printed in U.S.A.
First U.S. Edition: November 2022

To my kind sons, Joe and Kel,
and to all who choose the path of kindness.

Contents

Introduction

The firefly flicker of candlelight and the sweet sound of soft singing added a dreamlike quality to the summer night as three hundred and fifty singers carrying luminaria encircled the reflecting pool in the lush formal gardens of Portland's Lewis and Clark College. The 2017 annual gathering of Threshold Choir International (TCI) was a feast of ceremony, outstanding options for educational workshops, and an embarrassment of riches in talent and song offerings. Bonded by our dedication to the mission of gently singing to the dying, these were my people. I didn't want the All Choir Gathering to end.

A wild idea popped into my head during the morning meeting the next day, and, lit with excitement, I couldn't wait to share it. In front of bedside singers from around the globe, I announced that I would retire in a year, give up my apartment, buy an RV, and tour Threshold Choir chapters around the country. I didn't say I was *considering* the project, or that this was a journey I *hoped* to make, I declared that in a year's time, I would do this thing.

Saying the plan out loud for the first time, I was struck by how difficult it would be to leave my life in Pacific Grove, California; the Threshold Choir chapter there, the volunteer activities that had been my passion for over a decade, and the marvel of Monterey Bay. I shared that, too. Tears formed when I spoke of how important the Threshold Choir community is to me, and I heard myself say, "I need you." That uncharacteristic admission would be my saving grace. At the time, I had no idea how much I would depend on the kind and generous support received from the bedside singers in that room, and those I would meet traveling in the US and Canada.

The impulsive announcement received an ecstatic response at the gathering. The invitations I received made it clear that visiting Threshold Choir chapters is a dream shared by many in this organization. Most considered themselves unable to tour on the scale I was proposing due to family responsibilities, jobs, health, financial status, or fear of the unknown, and this only increased their excitement for the idea.

For me, the prospect of carrying songs and sharing insights and stories gathered while traveling offered a way to show up for those who provide this sacred service. I was excited about the opportunity to carry songs, learn new songs, and observe the variety of compassionate leadership models practiced by each chapter. The prospect of having Threshold Choir family as my touchstone in communities around the US and Canada, helped me overcome any fears I had about making the journey alone. I also looked forward to paying tribute to this vital work by writing about the beauty of singing at bedsides and the culture of kindness and connection it promotes.

My plan to chase a dream around the country may not have been the most sensible choice for someone facing financial uncertainty. I had reached retirement age, but like so many considering leaving the workforce, it was unclear how I would navigate the treacherous waters of living on Social Security retirement while rent, utilities, food, and other expenses spiral upward.

Changes in staffing had significantly increased the workload and stress level of my job at the nonprofit where I had been working for ten years. The essential work of providing affordable housing for unhoused adults with mental illness, and the compliance required by the multiple sources of government funding tapped to achieve that goal, often called for ten to twelve hour work days. The demands of my job did not feel healthy anymore, and I was too old and too burned-out to look for other meaningful employment. At the same time, my landlord's plan to make upgrades to my apartment and increase the monthly rent to an amount "more in line with the market," added to the pressure.

Emerging health issues, waining joie de vivre, and a memory that was slowing down were clear indicators that my window for this sort of undertaking was closing. With the image of Lil, the heroic elderly waitress at my first restaurant job, skillfully balancing five heavy dinner platters on her slender arms while beads of sweat dripped from the end of her nose still fresh in my mind, I was determined not to squander the long-awaited gift of my "golden years" struggling to keep up with an unmanageable workload.

When the gravity of my very public commitment began to sink in, I realized a song was the catalyst. At Song Village a month earlier, Karly Loveling[1] led *"I'm a Wild One Now,"* a delightfully whimsical song that made me laugh, and awakened the free spirit that was sleeping within me. The song triggered a longing to rewild, a shift that would require letting go of what no longer served me to give myself wholly to my passion for service, song, and the awe and wonder to be found in the natural world. I believe in the power of song.

I'm a Wild One Now

by Sage Marie Stanzler, Written 2012, © 2019

Let the sun shine down and warm my bones
Let the birds and the bees come and take my clothes
Cause I'm a wild one now made of wind and rain
I'm wild and I ain't going back again.

Let the moon shine down and cleanse my soul
Let the wolves and the owls come and tend my coals
Cause I'm a wild one now made of stars and dreams
I'm wild and I'm part of everything.

Let the stars shine down and cleanse my heart
Let the beaver and the bear teach me of their art
Cause I'm a wild one now made of fat and fish
The tending of the wild is my greatest wish.

The timing of the 33,000-mile journey was remarkable. I completed the pilgrimage four months before the COVID-19 pandemic would shut down the nation and the world. I traveled when campgrounds and city, county, state, and national parks were open, Threshold Choirs were meeting regularly, and choir members I didn't know greeted me with hugs. Before COVID-19 made singing dangerous, I participated in singing retreats, sang with community choruses, and sang with Threshold Choir chapters as they came together to practice in private homes, care facilities, and churches. I was invited to sing at bedsides in hospitals, and assisted living and hospice facilities.

Song was my one companion on this journey, the bridge that carried me from solitude to belonging. The knowledge that no matter where I traveled I was no more than a few days' drive from a Threshold Choir chapter gave me the confidence I needed to stretch my wings. Intentionally pushing the limits of solitude to experience the full force of that brilliant human ache for connection, I may never have felt so alive or so alone.

My personal dive into the hunger of the soul that comes of time spent in solitude is an exploration of feelings we would all experience sheltering-in-place under the threat of COVID-19. The mortality that we share is another topic in this book that the pandemic moved to the forefront of our minds.

The gift of purpose, the songs, the wonder of the outer and inner landscapes I navigated, and the kindness and belonging I encountered along the way shimmer within me, an exquisite dream I am compelled to write down before it is forgotten. In sharing the memories, stories and the wisdom shared with me, last names are only used to credit direct quotes and songs. Out of respect for their families, I have changed the names of those we sang home. Please know that song lyrics in this book are printed with the permission of the songwriters.

This bow to the wisdom of song comes of my yearning to share my personal journey and does not represent the views of the Threshold Choir International organization, Wholehearted Chorus, or any of the singing groups or individuals mentioned here.

It is the best gift to know why you are here ... know what your purpose is.

Kate Munger
Founder, Threshold Choir International

CHAPTER 1
A Call to Service

Radiant with hope, Mick sat tall in his wheelchair as he enthusiastically welcomed us to his apartment to sing for the first time. With his devoted sweetheart holding his hand, and three of his friends shyly observing from the couch, a quiet reverence filled his crowded living room. Knowing that Mick was determined to defeat his recurring cancer, and that despite his doctor's recommendation, he had refused hospice care, Susan, Jill, and I chose songs from the Threshold Choir repertoire that would support his desire to hold onto hope.

Listening intently to each word, Mick turned to his girlfriend again and again to silently mouth phrases of the songs that deeply touched him; "Don't Give Up," "Deeply Loved," and "Sending You Light." In the resonant silence between the songs few words were spoken, except that I remember hearing him whisper, "Miracles happen."

The Threshold Choir of Pacific Grove had been singing to hospice patients and community members for four years when we first visited Mick. In that time, we had seen the gift Kate Munger[2] has dubbed "Kindness made audible" open hearts to tears, laughter, joy, and sorrow. Mick found inspiration in the singing, drinking in the offerings as if he had a deep thirst. His gratitude was a shining light so intense, it brings tears to my eyes to think of it, even now. If I wasn't fully committed to the service by the time we sang to Mick, after that touching thirty-minute sing, I knew I wanted to devote myself to this work.

The first meeting of Threshold Choir in El Cerrito, California, on March 21, 2000, was "magical" according to Kate. "The minute I started this work, I knew that everything I had done before had been in preparation for this. All I had to do was take the next step." The next step was to gather women to sing together (the choir started with women's voices, but now welcomes all singers), teach songs of compassion and support, many of them written by Kate specifically for bedside singing, and share what it means to sing for the dying.

She taught prayerful presence, not performance. Sung softly, the simple, chant-like songs are meant to float like "a feather on the breath of God," in the words of Saint Hildegard von Bingen. Choir members learn to blend their voices together in unison and sweet harmonies to create one voice, in service. Kate assembled an angel choir.

Susan Graves is one of the fifteen singers who attended that first meeting when Kate "gathered people to illuminate their minds and hearts with this wild idea." Susan confirmed the magic of that meeting saying there was stardust in the room, and all who were present "knew this thing was going to take off because it was so pure. It was life-changing for me."

Leaving that fateful gathering, Susan said she felt elevated as if she were in an altered state. Driving home at 10:30 that night, she stopped when she spotted an elderly man stooped over a walker on the sidewalk. When she asked if he was all right, he told her he was waiting for his bus. Feeling as if the Threshold Choir meeting she attended that night had left her with "angel wings," she offered him

2

a ride home because there was no way she could leave him at the side of the road. Helping him climb into the car and getting his walker and his belongings packed inside was not easy, and she said he talked non-stop all the way to his Oakland apartment.

Learning he had no family and his only friends were city bus drivers, Susan promised to visit him again, thus beginning five years of Tuesday evening visits she calls her *"Tuesdays with Morrie"* evenings.[3] When his health deteriorated, Susan's visits with her new friend continued at his nursing home, and in time, she began working there. As a result of that first meeting, "I let this little man into my life." She said Threshold Choir broke her heart open. It has also influenced Susan's professional choices, lighting the way to the social work and counseling that has added meaning to her life.

Some call Kate Munger a saint. I consider her an angel. Her generosity, calm demeanor, and the ceramic angel necklace she wears reinforce that image. She discovered the beauty of singing at bedsides in 1990 while caring for a friend who was in a coma. Terrified to spend time sitting with the dying man, "I did what I always did when I was afraid, I sang a song that gave me courage." The singing was a balm that calmed Kate, and the agitated, comatose patient. "I felt as if I had given generously of my essence to my dear friend." Kate realized that she was onto something.

She applied herself to a study of music, songwriting, and using technology to reach out to community and launched Threshold Choir ten years later. The work establishing the choir required drive, literally. For years, Kate directed the practices of the six chapters she started in the San Francisco area and Santa Cruz, and led a singing circle for the women incarcerated at the Marin County Jail with Threshold Choir singers from around the Bay Area. As interest in bedside singing swelled, Kate was invited to give presentations at hospice conferences and help new chapters get started around the country. She told me she was driving 33,000 miles each year. I know just how far that is because, coincidentally, that is how many miles I put on my camper van in my quest to travel the US visiting Threshold Choirs.

Demand for the offering continued to grow as news spread about this heartfelt service rooted in tradition. Financial support for Kate's time and travel expenses came in the form of donations placed in the velvet pouch she passed at the practices and gatherings she led. She asked only for donations that are "Generous, affordable and personally significant." She found the work "an honor and a joy."

Song Medicine

The knowledge that music is medicine is not new. Doctors who play Sufi music on traditional flutes to quiet anxiety, slow heart rates, and increase the oxygen saturation levels of patients at Memorial Hospital in Istanbul point out that music has been used as a healing modality in Turkey since the Ottoman Empire.[4] Researchers around the world are finding that patients, including premature infants, feel reduced pain from IV injections while listening to soothing music, especially live music.[5] Breakthroughs using music

4

in the treatment of Parkinson's and Alzheimer's disease are widely acknowledged.

In addition to the medical benefits, music has been proven to provide emotional support. It eases anxiety and releases endorphins by lowering the stress hormone, cortisol.[6] The medicinal value of music has earned mainstream recognition over the past few decades, and now most large hospitals in the US employ Music Therapists to sing and make beautiful music at bedsides with harps, guitars, and flutes.

I am not a scientist, a medical professional, or a Music Therapist, but as a bedside singer with Threshold Choir, I have many times witnessed how singing calms those who are suffering and soothes the passage to the other side for the dying and their loved ones. The human voice has the ability to engage and comfort. I have seen late stage Parkinson's patients relax and unfold fists, arms, and bent torsos when we sang to them, cease involuntary moaning, and smile and sway with the music. A stroke victim frustrated that he could not communicate cried tears of joy when he found himself singing along to the familiar songs we brought to his bedside. Alzheimer's and dementia patients can remember song lyrics when their children's names may escape them.

I am eternally grateful for the opportunity to sing at bedsides with Threshold Choir. Singing is a gift for both the listener and the singer, and singing for those at the tender moments at the end of life is an extraordinary privilege. It is also a potent reminder of the mortality that we all share. In *Tuesdays With Morrie,*

Morrie Schwartz's recipe for living a meaningful life is: "Devote yourself to loving others, devote yourself to your community around you, and devote yourself to creating something that gives you purpose and meaning."[7] Singing at bedsides with Threshold Choir has opened the door to that kind of meaningful life.

A Need to Sing

Kate Munger was someone I needed to meet. She was a presenter at the 2006 singing retreat that I attended in the second year of working to reclaim the singing voice lost to me when I was diagnosed with vocal cord paralysis. For twelve months, the virus, a form of Bell's Palsy, made speaking difficult and singing impossible. Working with a speech therapist, I learned to take a breath after every two words to have enough support to push the functioning vocal cord close enough to the paralyzed side of my larynx to create sound. Words came, often in a whisper, but I could not sing or sustain a pitch. Losing the ability to sing was comparable to losing the ability to laugh, with all of its physical and emotional elements.

Fortunately, my condition was temporary. Once the virus had run its yearlong course, I could sing, but I was left with a range reduced to barely one octave, a wobbling vibrato that made it difficult to stay on pitch, and my voice regularly cracked and cut out when I tried to sing. No one could tell me what kind of lasting damage the prolonged strain had caused, only time and work to strengthen the atrophied muscles of the larynx would reveal the extent of damage. The unpleasant sounds that emerged when I tried to sing were a bitter pill to swallow.

Singing was my first passion, my one talent. The fact that my family did not believe music studies to be worthwhile did not stop me. I sang to the birds, the hills, and the creeks, and unbeknownst to my parents, sang Christmas carols at strangers' doors, by myself, receiving a cache of holiday treats from bewildered neighbors. In fourth and fifth grade, I led my school in patriotic song at the flag-raising ceremony each morning (this was the 1950s, friends), led songs at Girl Scout campfires, and led Scout songs for the families attending my brother's monthly Cub Scout Pack meetings.

Blessed with the ability to sing from a place of pure joy, judgment was suspended, I was not troubled by perfection. With no training, I was oblivious to the mistakes I made, I trusted my voice to know what to do. As a teen in the 1960s, I spent my free time gathered with friends in public parks blissfully singing folk songs that gave voice to our desires and concerns. We hitchhiked to Griffith Park love-ins on Sundays to sing and dance in larger circles. I was in my thirties when I took my first voice lessons, followed by study with a number of teachers and six years of weekly singing classes. I was experimenting with the playful interaction of vocal improvisation in community singing circles when vocal cord paralysis struck.

At the singing retreat in the Santa Cruz mountains, my voice frequently faltered, cut out, and required regular rests. Kate was an inspiration; the songs she shared brought tears, and the idea of offering sacred song at the bedsides of the dying was a service that called to me on many levels. Kate sang softly, encouraging the group to listen to each other and blend voices in what she calls "lullaby singing."

This was something I could do, even with the diminished singing voice I was struggling to love.

After three more years of vocal work, I felt ready to join Threshold Choir. Even though I no longer had the range or resonant sound I once had, I met the requirements for singing with this choir: be able to carry a tune; be able to hold your own part (or sincerely want to learn to); be able to sing softly and blend your voice with others (or sincerely want to learn); be able to communicate kindness with your voice.

I drove out of town to attend weekly practices with other choirs for a full year before starting a chapter in my community. In April of 2010, the Threshold Choir of Pacific Grove met for the first time, with Kate, and members of the Santa Cruz and Aromas chapters in attendance to support the effort to launch the new chapter.

At the weekly practices that followed, our new choir studied the repertoire, practiced harmonies, and prepared for coming face-to-face with the realities of death. We worked to develop within ourselves a presence that has no expectations or desire to draw attention to itself, leaning into the messages of the songs for the non-judgmental generosity of heart we wished to bring to bedsides. The use of song, silence, and breath as tools to ground and center is a well I continue to drink from, particularly vital when singing at a bedside after the demands of a hectic day.

After a year of practice and training, the Threshold Choir of Pacific Grove began singing for friends, and friends of friends within our community. It took two years before we were confident enough to offer singing to our local hospice organization. Only three of us completed the hospice training and committed to the TB testing and annual competency tests and flu shots required of volunteers with the Hospice of the Central Coast. We had enough singers for the three-part harmonies. Suzan, Jill, and I regularly brought songs to the bedsides of hospice patients and others in need of support. We could count on each other to show up for every practice and bedside sing grateful for the opportunity to be of service.

Under Kate's loving leadership, the choir continued to grow. When the undertaking became too much for one person to manage, a website was developed, an Executive Director was hired, and members were asked for annual donations to support the administration of the organization. By 2012, Threshold Choir was a 501(c)3 non-profit organization one hundred chapters strong and growing. Experienced directors help new chapters launch, and take on the role of coaches.

Prior to COVID, over 2,000 singers and more than 200 Threshold Choir chapters were actively singing for those facing death, grief, and suffering around the world, and the movement continues to grow as chapters regroup after the pandemic driven transition to Zoom.

Meadow Magic.

CHAPTER 2

Manifesting the Dream

On August 15, 2018, fourteen months after announcing my wild idea at the All Choir Gathering, I moved from my apartment to my home on wheels, a twenty-year-old Roadtrek RV van conversion purchased after months searching online for an RV that I could afford. The clean exterior with wave-like trim the color of Monterey Bay on a sunny day and the cozy ship-like cabin with oak cabinets and spa-aqua upholstery, had me at first sight. The skylights, abundance of windows, toilet, heater, hot and cold running water, stove, and refrigerator were everything I needed to comfortably live on the road. The fact that all of this fits into a nineteen-foot-long van so perfectly is some kind of magic trick.

Although the Roadtrek is small for an RV, driving a Toyota Corolla for decades had not prepared me for the demands of driving the extended van. Taking my prize home, a strong crosswind sent the tall vehicle veering towards traffic in the next lane of Pacific Coast Highway. Attempting to stay the course, I overcorrected, and continued to overcorrect, jerking the vehicle back and forth in my lane until I regained control. Jill was following close behind, and she was frightened seeing me flailing about on the highway. It scared me too, but I was determined that fear wouldn't get in the way of my plans. Prior to leaving on the journey, I honed my van driving skills, and with assistance from the back-up camera, practiced back-in parking.

Letting Go

Working long hours in my final months of employment left me only two weeks to liquidate my possessions and vacate my apartment. I needed that looming deadline, and the help of friends, to pull it off. Before I could let go, I meticulously examined each photo, CD, and DVD, each piece of clothing and jewelry, and every little thing stored on every shelf, in every cabinet and drawer, and stuffed into every closet. Anything that wasn't essential for life on the road had to go. Paying for storage was not an option.

There was little time for sleep during those final days of clearing out the apartment. I had 1,500 photos scanned and threw away the prints, all of them. I burned boxes of journals and scraps of paper with fifty years of notes, releasing them as smoke. I photographed my favorite things: the rugs, the exquisite Chinese desk, the art, and the Tony Lama cowboy hat I wore to the Angola Prison Rodeo in Louisiana, capturing the delight of friends and strangers as they took possession of the treasures. Finding someone to take on the burden of twelve settings of china ended decades of packing and transporting the impractical dishware with each move. The faux jade statue of the Goddess Quan Yin pouring water for a thirsty dog at her feet was one of the objects I placed in a friend's gift box, only to remove it and put it back many times as I struggled to let it go. At the last minute, my prized collection of rocks and shells found a home with a friend.

My friend, Sandor, built a cabinet to replace a second passenger seat that was taking up critical space, making room in the van for the books I could not part

with, art materials, and the CDs and DVDs I wanted
to carry. Remarkably, the cabinet he added matched the
oak interior perfectly, right down to the brass door
handle. It became an essential part of my "office." With
the passenger seat swiveled around to face the cabinet,
and my drop down table in place, I had a little desk
the same size as the desk used by Emily Dickinson to
write volumes of inspirational poetry in her famous bedroom in Amherst, Massachusetts.

My Office.

The time and effort required to sort through my
belongings and make the hard choices about what I could
and could not keep gave me a better understanding of the
terrible hardship suffered by those who lose everything to

fires, floods, hurricanes, and tornadoes, with no time for the sorting process that was so important to me.

The grief resulting from my choice to downsize was unexpected. Dazed by the transformation, I frequently referred to the digital images of the things I had sold and given away to help get my bearings during the first few months of my travels. As anxious as I was to let go of the trappings of the material world, the notion that our lives are measured by our possessions is hard to shake. I thought about this each time I entered a home embellished with personal treasures, art, and decorations.

Choosing to live on Social Security at one-third my salary, I would not be resuming the lifestyle I led with full-time employment income. According to Hindu teachings, I was graduating from *Grihastha* (householder) to the next stage of life, *Vanaprastha* (retired), a time for detachment, self-discovery, and service that translates as "retiring to the forest."

The purge was also part of my preparation for death. This was my *döstädning,* the Swedish death cleaning meant to prevent leaving a mess behind for family to sort out. I was excited about starting my new life Marie Kondo clean.

With the opportunity to spend two full weeks making the two-day drive along the coast from Central California to my son's small farm on the central coast of Oregon, I initiated the slow and deep travel practice that would serve me well on this adventure. Always choosing the scenic route, I made frequent stops to explore the world unfolding around me. It was my intention to let wonder be my guide. On the way north, I glamped in my room with a view, sleeping in a bed with 600-thread-count sheets in the same places where I slept on the ground in tents over the years. The toilet conveniently located in a cabinet in my "bedroom" was the ultimate luxury, accommodating my middle-of-the-night pee with ease and grace. After that convenience, there is no going back to the exercise of putting on shoes and a jacket in the dark of night to stumble out of a tent and find a place to squat and pee that is sufficiently private, far from poison oak, and away from walkways where a visible wet mark would be evident to passersby in the morning light, or repeat the struggle to keep the pajama pants pulled down around my knees from getting dirty, or worse yet, wet with pee.

Fire Scars

I arrived in Sonoma Valley ten months after the devastating Sonoma Complex firestorms that destroyed 5,600 structures in Sonoma and Lake Counties in October 2017. The weight of the trauma hung in the air like a dark cloud. Fire destroyed close to fifty percent of the homes in the enclave of Glen Ellen, where I lived for sixteen years in the shadow of Sonoma Mountain. The home of former next-door neighbors was one of few spared on Warm Springs Road, and Ritch and Margie wasted no time moving three trailers onto their property to house displaced neighbors while they rebuilt, an undertaking that would take more than two years.

In Kenwood, ninety-seven-year-old Marj Davis had ten minutes to escape before her home was completely consumed by fire. She expressed little concern for her lost material possessions, what did concern her was the loss of the fawn care manual, *Black-tailed Fawns-Care in Captivity,* that she had just updated. She jumped right into a rewrite, and within ten months of losing her home, she had completed a new update. We visited in the one room cabin where she and her husband set up camp amid the charred oaks in their old neighborhood. We sang "Que Sera, Sera" together at her dining room table and before we said goodbye, I thanked her for her dedication with Penelope Salinger's "Dear One."

The fires that summer also claimed the home of a friend in Redding and would take the entire town of Paradise in November. Smoke followed me north, and in the orange glow of a smoke enhanced sunset, I arrived at my campsite at Richardson's Grove State Park in Northern California's Humboldt County.

Solo Date Night

Alone in a sacred forest of giant redwoods, I chose to celebrate the adventure that was unfolding with a solo "date night." Under the tall trees, I prepared a dinner of curried lentils and rice on my camp stove, set the picnic table with a colorful Indian print tablecloth and enameled dishes, and ate by candlelight as day gave way to night. The curry inspired me to keep the theme going with the sumptuous Mira Nair film, *Monsoon Wedding,* from the collection of DVDs I brought along to watch on my computer after dark.

The next day started with Laurence Cole's cheerful song of praise to the new day, "Oh Morning," but my ecstatic mood quickly changed when I discovered a persistent water drip coming from one of the connections under the vehicle. As it turns out, the tanks and tangle of plumbing attached to the undercarriage of the van can produce leaks and malfunctions that I hadn't considered. As convenient as it is to travel with a toilet and hot and cold running water, I knew nothing of the systems that keep those conveniences working.

When I reached Eureka, easygoing Al, a seasoned RV mechanic in muddy overalls, replaced the leaking PVC connection in no time. He also came up with a solution for the broken latch on the refrigerator door where my Super Glue fix had failed. I left Al with the song, "I Wish That I Could Show You."

Overwhelmed by the van's operating systems, I put off emptying the holding tanks (greywater from the sink, and black water from the toilet) until I reached my son's farm. Joe accompanied me to the RV dump site in his town, offering the support I needed to take on the task for the first time. Learning to empty the holding tanks was the first step, overcoming my aversion to a public viewing of my excrement at dump sites, was something else again.

Three days after my reunion with Joe and his wife, Gretchen, I left the Roadtrek at their farm on the Oregon coast to fly to Ireland. The trip had been at the top of my bucket list for decades, and to ensure it would come to pass, I planned and paid for it before retiring. While I spent the month of September immersed in the sacred sites, music, poetry, and death rituals of the home of my ancestors, generous Joe, a master electrician and skilled handyman, equipped the van with solar power.

On my return from Ireland, Joe took on the role of RV mentor, answering questions and advising me on repairs by phone as I traveled. Joe and I had acknowledged the transfer of guardianship that takes place between parents and adult children long ago when he commented on the role reversal as he reached across the table to wipe salsa from my chin at a Mexican restaurant.

Joe and Gretchen's farm on the Oregon coast would serve as the launching pad for my Threshold Choir tour in the Pacific Northwest.

Farm Friends.

CHAPTER 3

Singing at the Threshold

A practice in Corvallis, Oregon, on October 7, 2018, would be my first choir visit. The Heart of the Valley Threshold Singers were preparing for their first hospice sing when I visited. The chapter had been singing together for one year. The director, Susan, kindly made time available at the practice for me to introduce "Trees Grow Slow," the Laurence Cole song I carried to nearly every choir and community singing circle stop I made as I traveled around the country.

The first choir practice of my journey was also my first night camping in a choir member's driveway. Sarah and David graciously provided a place to park, good company, shared meals, and poetry. Because sleeping in a vehicle on the street is illegal, I would depend on driveway camping to reduce the expense of campgrounds each night. Without much financial cushion, accomplishing my mission would require keeping costs at a minimum. I budgeted for a maximum monthly camping expenditure of $300, about ten nights at no-frills campgrounds. Most nights on the road required scouting for free parking. The time spent with those kind driveway hosts would turn out to be the highlight of my adventure.

Bringing Death into the Conversation

One of the members of the Corvallis chapter is an activist working to promote Death with Dignity legislation around the country. After decades of defeated bills aimed at decriminalizing assisted death, in 1997, Oregon was the first state to legislate the right. As of December 2022, ten states and the District of Columbia have legalized physician-assisted death for the terminally ill. The End of Life Option Act was signed into law in California in October 2015, a year after a determined thirty-year-old with terminal brain cancer found it necessary to move from California to Oregon in her final weeks of life for the right to choose not to prolong her suffering.

In states where physician-assisted death is legal, the right is extended only to those who obtain verifications of impending death from doctors, have the capacity to confirm their choice up to the final moment and can self-administer the final dose of the prescribed medication, and can afford the expensive drugs approved for the process. Organizations like the Final Exit Network help those without access to medically assisted death, and provide education about methods for self-deliverance that are within the law. Offering a choice of death with dignity is the intention of the legislation and help groups.

In Canada, MAID (Medical Assistance in Dying) is covered by the universal medical insurance coverage, but it is not without controversy. Elaine Andrews, the director of the London Ontario Threshold Choir told of her choir's first experience singing for a patient who had chosen MAID. As a Christian, she struggles with the end-of-life choice, as did other members of the chapter. Recognizing that not all singers would be comfortable witnessing this type of death, she made it clear that they were free to choose whether or not they wished to participate in the bedside sing. She wanted the singers to know, "We are not making the minds up for these people, but we could offer prayer and comfort."

According to Elaine, "When we sang for the gentleman who received MAID, we not only sang for him, we sang for his family, for his wife, for his children and grandchildren who were in the room. We sang for the clergy, the doctor, and his nursing support. We sang songs of comfort, gratitude, and songs of faith. We sang as the wife lay in bed with her husband and they held one another. This is our role. I can assure you that when a palliative patient applies for MAID, the family is not always (rarely) in agreement with the decision. We sing for all of them."

And they didn't stop there, "When he was being wheeled out, we offered him an honor guard and we sang to him by the main entrance. We sang again to his family and to a large crowd that was mainly staff. There wasn't a dry eye present. We often forget the staff who have heavy hearts and have tears that need to be expressed."

Openness to the multitude of personal beliefs and choices of the dying, and the opportunity to offer service without judgment, are underlying principles of Threshold Choir that draw me to this service.

I Believe in Miracles

Within a week of joining Threshold Choir, I made the acquaintance of a man with an extraordinary approach to death. At a Death Salon I attended at the Center for Spiritual Awakening in March of 2009, Brit announced he was dying of congestive heart failure, and spoke of his excitement about being at this threshold of transformation. Continuing around the circle, we heard from a mother who recently lost a son, a woman caring for her husband with terminal cancer, and I told of my son's miraculous return after all signs of life had ceased.

Afterward, Brit and I set up a meeting to continue the discussion. Brit's eagerness to experience the great mystery intrigued me. The conversation at our first meeting in front of the fireplace in the lobby of the Monterey Plaza Hotel was a stimulating exchange that included personal stories, thoughts about faith, and what we had read about death and dying. We talked for six hours.

Brit wanted to know more about my dance with death after the Tehauntepec River in southern Mexico swallowed my son in 1974. I told him about traveling with my four-year-old son, my friend, Theodora, and her four-year-old son, and our fateful stop in the town of Tehauntepec in the Sierra Madre mountains south of Oaxaca. After a month of traveling in the deeply patriarchal country, we were astounded by this town's matriarchal society and decided to stay for a few days before continuing on to Lake Atitlan in Guatemala. The Tehuanas, striking in the elaborately embroidered velvet costumes made famous by Frida Kahlo, are well known as *curanderas* with exceptional healing abilities.

Befriended by a young man who wanted to practice his English, we accepted Mario's offer to take us to the local swimming hole, a bend in the Tehuantepec River that was a center of activity for the people of this town. The boys had been playing in the shallow water for some time when the screams of women washing clothes at the riverbank alerted me that Theodora's son, Gabe, was floundering on the surface of a pool downstream. His head had dropped below the water by the time I reached him and swam him to shore. Throwing him over my shoulder to climb up the riverbank made him vomit and start breathing again.

With no time to waste, I began a desperate search for my son. Calling out for help, I heard again and again that no one had seen another boy. News spread, and townspeople flocked to the scene where, we later learned, drownings were common. Aware that Joe's survival was less and less likely with each passing moment, I frantically ran back and forth searching for him in the trash-littered water. At some point during the search, I was struck by the most desolate feeling of being alone, empty, without hope.

Miraculously, two villagers wearing diving masks jumped from a bluff above a deep pool to recover Joe's lifeless, bloated body from the bottom of the river, twenty minutes after the search began. When I reached him, Theodora was cradling Joe in her outstretched arms while a traveler we had invited to join us earlier that day administered resuscitation. Joe was not responding.

Seeing my state of despair, Theodora had this advice, "Don't look at him that way, look at him smiling." Her words turned my thoughts to what a special being Joe was, how kind and loving, how wise beyond his years, and how deeply loved he was by all who knew him. At that instant, I received a message to put my hands on his chest. It was something like a whisper in my ear without sound. I interpreted it as instruction to apply compression to assist with the resuscitation, but that was not the message.

When I touched Joe's body, it was empty. The life force that was my son was not present. With my touch, I felt life return and he began breathing soft shallow breaths. Women washing clothes at the riverside and villagers who had gathered to help in the search dropped to their knees in prayer at the sight.

After four harrowing days barely clinging to life, Joe returned, body, mind, and soul. With clear eyes, wide awake, and able to speak for the first time since the rescue, he told me he wanted his mommy now. When I assured him I was there, he responded with a statement that remains a mystery to this day, "No, you know what I mean, I want my real mommy now."

My healthy, wise, creative, funny, and happily married son turned fifty in 2020. He remembers nothing of the river or the four days that followed. Having no conscious memory of the incident may have spared him the post-traumatic stress disorder that consumed me when we returned to California, and is with me still, to a lesser degree. The miracle that occurred, the gift of Joe's health, and the unexplainable lack of brain damage after so long underwater, were not lost on me, but the horror of Joe's drowning and the feeling that I had lost him tortured my days and nights.

Help came in the form of the story of a near death experience that a friend shared with me. Fred, a survivor of World War II, spoke about seeing soldiers around him dying as explosives bombarded the foxhole they occupied, and of the shell he saw coming for him, which he demonstrated with a diminishing whistle. He explained how his life flashed before him: first came regrets, then a tremendous calm, and finally, a yearning to let his loved ones know about the bliss he had found.

The explosive that hit Fred turned out to be a blank, and he told me that after finding such peace beyond, waking in a hospital bed knowing he would have to resume the strife and struggle of his life was a disappointment. He gave me a picture to replace the terrifying vision of Joe's suffocation by drowning that was playing over and over in my head. After hearing this story, I could imagine serenity coming over my sweet child as he found peace at the bottom of the river. Fred's story helped me turn my attention to gratitude for the miracle of Joe's return.

Death Curious

I took the life-changing event to be a hard-won gift of understanding that we are more than merely a body. Touching Joe's body empty, and feeling the return of his essence, whatever that may be, convinced me that there is more to us than flesh and bones. I know many people come to this awareness through their faith, I needed a hands-on experience to be convinced that spirit transcends our bodies. With that knowledge, how can one fear death?

The experience ignited a burning desire to learn about others' experiences with near death and the process of leaving one's body, a curiosity that is as strong today as it was in 1974 after witnessing the drowning incident. What is this force that dwells within us and where does it exist when our bodies can no longer offer a vessel for that entity? What lies beyond, and what is the meaning of Joe's request for his real mommy?

Inspired by the Mexican culture's continuing relationship with their ancestors, I returned to the land of miracles for extended visits and for Día de Los Muertos celebrations. The happy music of mariachi bands in the flower-adorned cemeteries where families congregate at gravesites to feast and celebrate deceased loved ones is confirmation that living in harmony with the ghosts of the dead can enhance our lives. The poet Margaret Atwood suggested that although we think it is the living who carry on when the dead are gone, it could be the other way around.

Curiosity about death led me to study the subject. *Life After Life,*[8] by Raymond Moody, MD, was the first book I found that gives credibility to stories of near death experiences. My focus became a magnet, drawing those with personal stories of an unseen world that supports our lives on earth like roots below the surface support the lives of trees. I listened in wonder to a young man expected to die after being shot in the chest by the police in a case of mistaken identity. He told of watching his surgery from above, looking down at his sliced open body in the operating room, and hearing the doctor give up on him before he made the choice to return. A woman told of losing her sister in the Oakland Hills firestorm of 1991 three hours after receiving an excited call from her explaining that their departed mother had appeared in a lucid dream, radiantly delivering an emphatic message to have no fear, everything would be fine.

These are stories no one could make up, stories that shine with the magic that emerges when the veil between worlds is lifted. I am a moth drawn to the light present in the sacred mysteries of death and dying. Seeking a way to share the potential these stories have to reassure and ease the fear of death, I began gathering people to share personal experiences in *Miracle of Death Story Circles*. We can find meaning and guidance in our encounters with death, the dying, and dreams of ancestors. Making space for conversations about death also reminds us to make the most of the time we have been given here.

Teachers

Brit's light shone brightly as he stood on the threshold of life and death, looking forward to what was to come. He embraced death as a state of grace. I learned that he had been dealing with congestive heart failure for eight years, had burned through five pacemakers, and been close to death many times. He regretted having to give up tango dancing. That was all I knew about his physical limitations and pain; they were subjects he did not choose to dwell on.

It was hard to believe Brit was close to death. At sixty years old he was bright, vibrant, and very much alive. When I asked if there were things he wanted to do with his remaining time, such as travel, he said that time had passed for him. He told of taking a trip to France with his sweetheart two years earlier, and of the massive heart attack that forced him to spend weeks in a Paris hospital.

At this time, he chose to stay close to home, living moment by moment, day by day. He considered every-thing perfect in his life and was truly elated about the promise of crossing over to the next realm. Not burdened with fear or apprehension, he believed death would be an opening to peace and time without end. Brit's source of strength and hope was his spirituality.

We met several times over the next four weeks, with each exchange lasting for hours. I shared "My Grateful Heart" and other songs I was learning at Threshold Choir practices. We discussed Buddhist principles, reincarnation and past lives, and considered the teachings of Deepak Chopra, Eckhart Tolle, and Ram Dass. Believing that we choose our destiny when we leave our bodies, Brit was a kid in a candy shop exploring the options.

Knowing his positivity would offer a different perspective for a friend deep in despair after a diagnosis of kidney failure, I arranged an afternoon tea for them to meet. When the day arrived and I called to finalize the plans, Brit's girlfriend, his "angel," answered the phone. She explained that Brit had peacefully crossed over that morning. I am grateful to have met this amazing teacher.

The memorial song I wrote for Brit pops into my head when I pass the beach near the Point Pinos Lighthouse that became our meeting place for hours of discussion about the unknowable, and the realm of possibilities that could be waiting for us after death.

Memorial for Brit
© 2009 Susie Joyce

We celebrate your freedom from worldly care and strife,
A journey you've prepared for all your life.
Everything is perfect, you knew this to be so,
That understanding helps us let you go.
Now when the sun is shining, and the angle is just right,
We can see you dancing, dancing in the light.
You're all around us, dancing in the light.

As secure as I am in my belief that we are more than a body, Marj, one of my closest friends, has a different understanding. She is now 102 years old, and more than ready for death to come. She believes that when she dies, that will be the end of her. Period. She wishes to pass quietly without fuss or notice and has asked that there is no ceremony to mark her passing. If we lived in a different time and place, she would walk into the woods to die among the wild creatures she so loves. For decades, she worked tirelessly to put the right team in place to carry on her work rescuing and releasing injured and orphaned fawns through the non-profit she founded, Wildlife Fawn Rescue. She is satisfied knowing her work is done here, the mission will continue.

Each time we meet, she reminds me it may be the last time we see each other, and tells me how much our friendship means to her. From her, I have learned much about unconditional love, and the vitality that comes of living an impassioned life of commitment and purpose. I have also learned that death is different for each of us. In the vast sea of faith, science, spirituality, atheism, and agnosticism that shapes humanity, we each approach death on our own terms.

Singing Each Other Home

Although beliefs about death may differ, bedside singers agree that it is a tremendous privilege to be present when someone is transitioning from life on this plane. Those close to their time teach us that when the minutiae of daily living loses importance, it is our love for one another that shines through.

Knowing how to support the dying with acceptance and compassion while experiencing our own emotional response requires training and focus on the mission. Rev. Linda Bryce, a Threshold Choir singer and end-of-life doula, has written a definitive book on that subject, *The Courage to Care, Being Fully Present with the Dying.*[9]

The Threshold Choir of Pacific Grove has provided bedside singing for hospice patients who passed within hours of our visit many times; none have died while we were singing. On those occasions when a patient in their final hours stopped breathing for a bit, giving us cause to think they had taken their last breath, we kept singing. Continuing the melodic flow of song to honor that moment of grace in transition calls on singers to be unfaltering in their purpose.

Threshold singers who have witnessed death while singing at bedsides told me they referred to the family in those moments, asking those in attendance if they want the singing to continue. They told of diligently balancing the offering they bring with the need to be sensitive to and respect the privacy of family members overcome with grief.

The director of the Napa Valley Threshold Choir, Sudie Pollack, described the three deaths she witnessed at bedsides with her choir as peaceful, with breath quieting and ceasing as the choir was singing. When leading a sing at the bedside of someone who is close to death, she feels "a responsibility to be in sync with the dying person, to pay close attention to their breathing. If this is to be their last breath, we want to be there for the family." Sudie explained that supporting the family requires helping singers stay centered so they don't become emotional in a way that would draw attention or disrupt the singing. It also means switching from singing "crossing over" songs that ease the passage, to singing songs of support "while the family finds themselves." At each of those bedsides, the singers finished the song they were singing for the patient when their breathing stopped before moving on to a song for the family. After that, she said, "There was nothing more we needed to do."

Following those deaths, Sudie guided the singers to back away from the bedside as family started to move towards their departed loved one. They stood in the background quietly singing a song for family members before exiting the room without a word. Validation for the insight to leave as they did came from the daughter of one of those patients. She told them she didn't know they had gone because singing continued to resonate in the room.

Even though we prepare ourselves for the inevitable outcome, witnessing death has an impact on all of us. Leaving the deathbed after the first death they witnessed, Sudie said choir members convened outside, out of sight of family, trembling as they released emotions they did not show at the bedside. Taken aback after singing at the second of two deaths that occurred on the same day, Sudie said choir members held one another, sharing the feelings that emerged "until we said all that we needed to say to each other." One singer's emotional acknowledgment, "It worked, what we do brings comfort," emerged after the son who so lovingly stroked his mother's hair as she passed told the singers how grateful he was for the choir's beautiful gift to his mother.

Penelope Salinger told of singing to a Spanish speaker who was close to her time. She explained that the Santa Barbara Threshold Singers often receive requests to sing in Spanish. They started the sing with, *"Como Puerto Seguro,"* a Spanish translation of Chris Williams' song, "Lullaby," and seeing how deeply moving this was for the family gathered at the bedside, they stayed with it for a while. Interrupting the silence that followed the song, the patient's sister was vehement in her request, "Sing it again!" When the singers resumed the requested song, they observed the dying woman's breathing slow, and then stop. At that point, Penelope said the singers moved away from the bed and sang softly in the background, "as the family grasped that their loved one had made her transition."

"As we regrouped in the lobby of the facility, we acknowledged feeling kind of stunned." Making their way to a choir practice that happened to be scheduled that evening Penelope reported, "It was such a blessing to be able to immediately share with the group what we had experienced. It was the first time that anyone from our choir had been on a bedside sing when someone crossed the threshold, and we felt grateful for the privilege of singing this woman home in her mother tongue."

Marti Mariette, singing with a group of Santa Cruz Threshold Singers, told of arriving to sing at a private home just after a patient died. She said a caregiver met them at the door, told them the patient had passed, and dismissed them by closing the door. Feeling "there was a need for our songs," they commenced singing quietly outside the door. After some time, Marti said she felt compelled to offer singing to the family, not having had an opportunity to speak to them before. She knocked, and when the door opened, offered the service directly to family members gathered in the room. The group was invited in, and they consoled the grateful family and the caregiver with song as they grieved.

Karen DeTore told of pausing with a group of singers outside a hospice patient's room as "we took a moment to put our hearts together." Entering the room, they found the patient's two grown daughters in a panic and gasping for air because their mother had just passed and they didn't know what to do. Asked if they would like to be sung to, the daughters agreed.

The singing calmed the grieving women, and Karen said it transformed the room into sacred space. They requested their mother's favorite song, and when they joined the singing it helped them remember the happy times together. The sisters confided they would not have experienced that tender goodbye if the singing had not been offered.

The wealth of beautiful stories and songs waiting to be heard fueled my desire to connect with as many bedside singers as I possibly could as I traveled. With so many chapters and so much territory to cover, I left Corvallis anxious for my next scheduled choir meet-up in Portland.

Breathtaking View at Smith Rock State Park.

CHAPTER 4

Choosing the Scenic Route

On my way north, I stopped at Skull Hollow Campground in central Oregon, a recommendation from Gretchen. As a dedicated trail runner who regularly explores the trails of the West with her dog, Scout, she has a wealth of information about places to camp. This campground is near spectacular Smith Rock State Park, a popular rock climbing destination in Oregon's high desert country. The park is known as one of the best climbing regions in the nation. Captivated by the breathtaking views of stone pinnacles and faces, and the gorge created by the me-andering Crooked River over eons of time, I spent a full day hiking, picnicking, and watching daredevil climbers.

Knowing I would likely not have another opportunity to see the wonders of this spectacular land, I gave my-self permission to detour from my mission to explore. The diversions could mean driving hundreds of miles out of the way to answer the call of the wild. Given a choice, I take the scenic route every time. For me, the journey has always been as important as the destination. Grounding myself in the natural world was the foun-dation I needed to engage in the mad rush of highways and cities as I traveled around the country.

Hummingbird Hands

Attending a choir practice in Portland, it was mesmerizing to see Kri direct the gifted Portland Threshold Singers with hummingbird hands that communicate in a language more effective than words. Her focus on attunement, along with the vocal fine-tuning offered by voice teachers in the group, have helped shape the polished sound of this outstanding choir. Maria, a member of the Portland chapter, offered friendship and a place to park overnight, and we spent hours sharing songs and conversations about art, independence, and loss at her kitchen table.

From Portland, I continued north, and after a night at a noisy rest stop on Interstate 5, caught a morning ferry to Bainbridge Island and my next Threshold Choir practice. Maneuvering my oversized vehicle into tight parking in the belly of a ferryboat for the first time was a test of my driving skills and my nerve. The still water of Puget Sound helped calm my anxiety.

After a night with a dazzling view of the Seattle skyline from my waterfront campsite at Fay State Park, a loud squeal developed in one of the front wheels of the van as I explored the island. As if being marooned on an island with car problems wasn't bad enough, the grating metal-on-metal shriek, along with California license plates, drew scornful "go back to where you came from" looks from locals. Fortunately, on Bainbridge Island I had Judy, the director of the Agate Pass Threshold Choir, and Deborah, a Bainbridge Island artist and singer I met online through Songleader Flight School, to direct me to a trustworthy repair shop. This was the first of what would be an endless run of mechanical troubles that would dog me on this journey. Every new noise had me searching for a repair shop that could accommodate the size of the vehicle, and a mechanic who was willing to tackle the repair without an advance appointment, do the job right the first time, complete the work in one day so I could sleep in the vehicle each night, and wouldn't take advantage of a desperate traveler by overcharging or selling me unnecessary repairs. On Bainbridge Island, I was directed to just such a mechanic.

The bridge connecting Bainbridge to the Olympic Peninsula makes this island unusual in Washington's archipelago, where most islanders rely on ferries for transportation to and from the mainland. Detouring from the scenic drive from Bainbridge to Port Townsend, I traveled inland to the Kitsap County Fairgrounds dump site. It was time to empty the holding tanks, and my app directed me to the only dump site in the area. Locating the unmarked pipe in the ground that serves as the sewer access was no easy task, and once found, a tall concrete curb made the process of emptying the tanks, without the assistance of gravity, exceedingly difficult. I ripped the sewer hose during the process. Without a functioning toilet and with no available campsites in the area, I stayed in a hotel in the waterfront marvel, Port Townsend, to wait for an appointment at an RV repair shop.

The delay meant I had to cancel a visit to the Evergreen Threshold Singers near Seattle, something that was exceeding disappointing for me. There was plenty to see in Port Townsend, but my attempts to connect with the Threshold Choir there failed. With the plumbing fixed, I backtracked to reach the Threshold Choir on Vashon Island. Driving back and forth, hither and thither, would define my journey as I racked up the miles to meet with chapters when they were practicing.

I entered the wooded refuge of Barb and Ken's

charming cabin-like home on little Vashon Island in a thick misty fog, and was greeted with a warm fire and a meal prepared with vegetables from their garden. I learned this is a favorite stop for Kate Munger, the first of many Threshold Choir stops that followed in her footsteps.

Barb, one of the many kindred spirits I would meet on this journey, is a long-time Threshold Choir singer who served on the organization's first Board of Directors. She is also a songwriter, a music therapist who plays harp for patients, and a knowledgeable camping enthusiast. On Vashon, I attended the chapter's community songbath offering and enjoyed new friendships, singing, etheric harp music, good food, hiking, and recommendations for campgrounds that Barb and Ken have explored throughout the western US.

Whidbey Island was my next destination, the third Threshold Choir on Washington State's off-the-beaten-path islands I would visit. I was invited to camp next to Lisa's charming waterfront home where eagles call from the treetops. The warm-smoked salmon she served, and the salad adorned with paper thin watermelon radish and cucumber slices was a meal I won't forget. We shared deeply personal stories and sang comforting songs to her sweet old dog; a beloved companion with an exhausted heart that would give out within days of my visit.

At a practice of the "leaderful" Whidbey Bedside Singers, I learned about their unique model of leadership. In place of a music director, members known as "song mothers" take responsibility for learning specific songs, teaching them to the group, and leading them at practices and bedsides.

The Black Ball Ferry carried me across the water to Victoria, and another Threshold Choir. This charming city on Canada's Vancouver Island is also a mecca for community singing. In 2004, Denis Donnelly and Shivon Robinsong established the Community Choir Leadership Training program that draws singers from around the globe. I learned that Denis toured with John O'Donohue, whose gravesite I visited on Ireland's untamed western shores just weeks before, and knows the musicians I toured with in Ireland.

Susannah, my Threshold Choir host in Victoria, also sings in community singing circles. She regularly opens her home to musicians participating in the leadership training program, and Ben and Brita stayed with her before I arrived. I had an opportunity to sing with the talented couple when they were invited to share their music with the Wholehearted Chorus. They were en route to the training, and Susannah's home, at the time.

Songs that Bring Tears

Susannah invited me to join her at a Gettin' Higher Choir singing circle that Laurence Cole was leading the evening I arrived. "Trees Grow Slow" was one of the songs we sang together that night. My first exposure to that song was in a singing circle Laurence led for the Wholehearted Chorus in Monterey. I couldn't hold back my tears. In the chorus of this song that honors trees, I hear a tribute to the gifts we leave behind when we die. It feels important to share that message. Asked for permission to sing the touching chorus of the song at bedsides, gracious Laurence said that he would be honored.

Trees Grow Slow
by Laurence Cole

Verse 1:

Sometimes we wonder, a worried wonder,
what more can we do. In all our longing to bring healing
to this land will we last long enough to see it through.
From all our giving, all our passion all our care,
when we're gone will something good be left behind.
Then we hear a voice from deep inside, sweet simple
words come to ease our minds.

Chorus

Trees grow slow and trees grow strong.
And trees sway with the wind their whole lives long.
And trees hold the ground as they reach for the sky.
And fallen trees still feed the seeds
they cast before they died.

Verse 2:

We wander to and fro, stay awhile then go,
burn more holes in our boots. In all our going what we
want to know will be our souls ever put down roots.
Is there a somewhere we'll know we're finally home,
feeling this is the place where we belong.
Then we hear a voice so clear and strong, turn off your
mind, listen to the song.

Chorus

Verse 3:

We let the fences fall, what stands between us all and
sense the veil thin. The dark raven calls and tilts his wing
and sends a bolt of wild wisdom through our skin.
The winter wren is thrilling out its songs and fills our

hearts up to the brim. The whole living world just
takes us in. One more time let the song begin.
Chorus

With five days until the Victoria chapter's practice, I explored that elegant city before driving north as far as Rathtrevor Provincial Park, a campground in an enchanted forest on the east coast of Vancouver Island.

The island-studded channel between the park and Canada's west coast was a short walk from camp, and the Strait of Georgia was still on the mornings I walked the timber-strewn beach searching, in vain, for orcas. The glassy surface of the water was broken only by the sleek dark backs of sea lions combing the sea for fish with a motion so smooth that barely a ripple appeared in their wake. A playful sea lion pup created the only interruption to the placid scene, raising splash after splash with dolphin leaps that launched its arched body clear out of the water. Someone spotted a cougar in camp the first night. Vancouver Island is home to the largest concentration of cougars in North America, in addition to grizzlies, wolves, and a whole host of wildlife. My only woodland creature sighting would be the scores of little black bunnies darting about the campground.

As cozy as the van was with its excellent heater, the long chilly nights of the dusky northern woods were lonely. There were times when the realization that I was facing another night on my own brought on a surge of panic. With no phone signal, no internet service, and no radio, I had to be comfortable with myself. Even as I seek the depth of intimacy with myself and nature that is only achieved in seclusion, making peace with solitude is challenging. This night, an aching void moved me to seek company at a friendly pub, where traditional Irish music and comfort food took the edge off the cold night. Finding nourishment in solitude would take practice.

Logistics

The high cost of gas and ferries in Canada, coupled with the timing of practices, meant I could not visit the Threshold Choir chapter farther north on Vancouver Island, or the chapters on the mainland in Vancouver, British Columbia. I was sorry to be missing the Sunshine Coast Threshold Choir, and the choir member who was the first to extend an invitation on the morning I announced my plan. For the first time, I grasped the reality that my fanciful dream to visit all of the Threshold Choir chapters in the US and southern Canada was not possible given my financial limitations. This was deeply disappointing. I traveled to about half of the chapters in the US during the fourteen-month pilgrimage.

Logistics turned out to be much more complicated and time-consuming than I had imagined. Before starting the trip, I plotted a circle around the country charting chapter locations, seasonal weather, and rainfall. After touring the Pacific Northwest, I would head south to avoid freezing weather in the winter. Traveling in a counterclockwise circle, I would spend spring on the East Coast, and in the summer, follow the most northern route across the country towards the West Coast. In reality, it wouldn't be that simple. Scheduling around choir practices that are held every two weeks was strategically and geographically challenging, the weather was not as predictable as I had hoped, and I neglected to consider tornadoes.

I used the directory on the Threshold Choir website to locate chapters, determine practice schedules and find contact information, which I entered on a spreadsheet. On another Excel spreadsheet, I tracked where I spent each night. I also kept a spreadsheet I call "Great Ideas" where I documented procedures used to hone skills and nurture the bonding and culture of caring that exists within chapters. Without the website, networking with chapters around the country would not have been possible. I am so very grateful to those members dedicated to keeping the organization connected and growing.

Sending Light

I returned to Victoria in time to join a practice of the Threshold Choir chapter there. The meeting I attended was dedicated to sending prayers, in the form of songs, to those who are suffering or otherwise in need. Kate introduced the ritual of asking members to share the names of those they wish to sing for, or to silently bring them into the circle, and I found it to be part of nearly every practice I visited.

Sending You Light
by Melanie DeMore

I am sending you light to heal you, to hold you.
I am sending you light to hold you in love.
Verse 1
No matter where you go, no matter where you've been,
You'll never walk alone. I feel you deep within.

Chorus
Verse 2
No matter what you feel or what you choose to show, I'm always there for you, so I want you to know that …
Chorus
Verse 3
I walk the path with you; go slow, dear one, don't hurry
I'll go just like you go; there is no need to worry.
Chorus

After three or four names, the group will sing the deeply felt lyrics of the chorus of "Sending You Light" for those brought into the circle with us. The focused intention is powerful. Healing song sent to support and comfort those we sing for also brings comfort to choir members. The offering may be the only gift we have to give to loved ones in need.

During this gathering in the living room of a member of the Victoria Threshold Choir, we sent healing songs vibrating through space and time, singing for acquaintances, friends, and family members suffering serious illnesses that included a brain tumor and cancer. When one of the members mentioned feeling overwhelmed and asked that we take a break to nourish ourselves before going on, it brought a sigh of relief. I was grateful for the reminder to take care of my own needs. In response to the request, the choir director conveyed an eloquent closing honoring those we had sung for. After stopping for a cup of tea and a few songs for ourselves, we resumed "sending light."

I left Victoria on the midday ferry while the city was

44

readying community bonfires to celebrate Halloween. It was hard to leave the vibrant city, and my new friend, Susannah, but I was determined to arrive in Seattle in time for a Día de Los Muertos celebration with the Seattle Threshold Singers on November 1st.

This intimate Día de Los Muertos ritual initiated by Robin, the dedicated director of three Threshold Choirs in the Seattle area, is one of many activities that bonds this chapter so closely. The annual ceremony brings choir members together in Robin's living room to share photos and stories of departed loved ones, and then the group sings a song chosen from the Threshold Choir repertoire, or a favorite that had special meaning in their life. I was grateful to have the lovely blended voices in the circle honor my father with "Deeply Loved."

Refuge in the Trees.

CHAPTER 5

Wonder Driven Wanda

With winter nipping at my heels and road signs recommending snow tires, it was time to leave Washington and head south. I stopped in Tacoma to spent a day with Adina, a dear friend and revered Scrabble maven from Pacific Grove. She thought my adventure courageous, and spoke of her fear of traveling alone. I shared the song, "I'm a Wild One Now," and told her how it inspired me to reclaim wonder and joy in my life.

Our conversation led me to the awareness that I made a conscious choice to be wonder driven, not fear driven. Once I had spoken those words, I recognized I had discovered a truth about myself, a truth that would become my mantra. The philosophy not only applied to the mission I had untaken, it also applied to my view of life, and death. Leaving Tacoma, the realization that my van is providing the means to seek wonder led to the name that had been eluding me. I would call her Wonder Driven Wanda; Wanda, for short.

Arrangements had been made for a stop in Portland where I would lead a Miracle of Death Story Circle at a choir member's home, a service I believe is much needed in our death-denying culture. I had planned to invite chapters to participate in the offering as I traveled, but I was moving too fast to make the advance arrangements such gatherings require. During the journey, Portland would be the only location where I would offer the circle for choir members to share their personal stories and the songs, poems, grief, fear, astonishment, tears, and laughter that surface when we speak of the great mystery.

After another night parked outside Maria's Portland home, and another pajama party at her dining table, I pressed on. Silver Falls State Park, a campground in the forests of eastern Oregon that was suggested by Barb from Vashon proved to be a worthwhile detour. The park's Trail of Ten Falls offers spectacular vistas, and the opportunity to hike behind an enormous waterfall. A rustic lodge at the park offered the warmth of a roaring fire, internet, hot drinks, and a welcoming ambiance.

Jan, the director of the Salem Threshold Singers, and her husband, Don, were my gracious driveway hosts in Salem. I was touched by their hospitality and by the sweetness of the love and respect that I felt in their home. The choir practice I attended included a voice lesson from an accomplished young musical theater performer and choir director.

Even though the dates didn't work for connecting with the Eugene Threshold Singers, I drove to Eugene's University of Oregon campus hoping to meet with my effervescent friend, Dr. Barbara Mossberg.[11] Dr. B is the former Poet in Residence of Pacific Grove with whom I collaborated producing poetry events during her five-year term. Event planning meetings were brilliant. Her home, The Poet's Perch, was the setting of the intimate soirees where she treated the four-person support team to poetry, Prosecco, and elaborate feasts, that on at least one occasion, featured a combination of sweet potatoes and mascarpone that came to her in a dream. She calls me "Susie Rejoice," and she always encourages me when I pipe in with, "I have a song for that." The Poetry

Flash Mob we assembled at an art opening at the Pacific Grove Art Center is just one example of the innovation born of those inspired dinner meetings. Dr. B's choice of Neruda's odes to salt, tomatoes, the potato, and the lemon delighted a crowd of unsuspecting art enthusiasts.

With her packed schedule of teaching, meeting with students, and supporting her beloved Oregon Ducks football team, I was honored that Barbara was able to carve out time for a breakfast meeting. She was ecstatic about my quest, and with the unrelenting enthusiasm she is known for, Dr. B gushed that the journey was worthy of a documentary film and an appearance on Oprah. My focus was more modest. I would be happy simply to complete my mission of circling the country visiting as many Threshold Choirs as I could.

The Gift of Libraries

When I stopped to spend time in Eugene's sparkling glass-walled downtown library, the sound of singing was unexpected. The music came from a room where a group of people with disabilities was singing out loud, joyfully abandoning standard hushed library etiquette. Visiting libraries around the country was one of the highlights of my journey. It does the heart good to know these benevolent public treasures are providing, at no cost, extensive collections of reading materials for all ages, along with computers and Wi-Fi for students and other patrons who would not otherwise have internet access. Libraries also offer a gathering place for community, including the unsheltered inhabitants of our communities. I depended on libraries for internet connection to schedule routes and choir visits, communicate with choir members, check emails, download audio books, and post the blogs I had begun writing.

My blog was a fix for the biggest challenge of solo travel: having no one with whom I could share the trials and triumphs of the journey. Blogging also allowed me to process all that I was experiencing and consider what it meant to me. It provided a way to slow things down. The writing generated donations to a PayPal account where Threshold Choir members, appreciative readers and generous friends made contributions for gas and repairs. As long as I could keep my laptop battery charged, I could write anywhere, but posting those blogs required the internet connection available at public libraries.

It was fun to ferret out libraries, from the humble to the grand. I especially enjoyed locating historic Carnegie libraries constructed around the country between 1883 and 1929. One of those elegant structures graces downtown Pacific Grove. I saw libraries housed in lavish civic buildings that serve as community centers, like the public library in Tallahassee, Florida, where a volunteer assisted with my income tax filing (no simple task when you're on the road). In a residential neighborhood in Ann Arbor, Michigan, I spent time at a library housed in vacated retail space in a shopping mall. This seemed odd until I considered how convenient this was for residents of the neighborhood with plenty of parking and an adjoining café. At a modest library that occupies a small house donated to the town of Mendocino, California, even the wall space in the bathroom is equipped with floor-to-ceiling shelves to house the generous collection of books.

You Don't Own This

A forecast of below-freezing overnight temperatures forced me to abandon Eugene for the Oregon coast where the influence of the ocean keeps temperatures mild. With water tanks and plumbing onboard, freezing temperatures are not friendly to RVs.

I camped at Lagoon Park near the coastal town of Florence, where a lavish show of twinkling stars pierced the black bowl of night sky. When the moon rose over the tree tops, I caught sight of an enchanting ritual unfolding. Standing tall on slender legs, the coastal pines were performing an elegant dance with the wind; bowing greenery-crowned heads to their invisible partner, circling, and then returning to their upright starting position with grace and ease.

After so many years living in apartments where the landlord's liabilities result in blazing lights strategically placed everywhere darkness might be hiding, I crave dark nights. Even in campgrounds, many campers choose to light up the night with string lights and solar lighting that mask the glories of the night sky. I often wonder about the prevailing fear of darkness. Is it a holdover from cave-dwelling days when night prowling predators had a clear advantage over humans with poor night vision?

With weeks before my next scheduled Threshold Choir practice in Northern California. I drove up and down the rugged coastline of Oregon, returned to Joe and Gretchen's farm, and tackled some needed van repairs. North of Lincoln City, I stopped at picturesque small towns, lazy estuaries and busy fishing ports for a closer look. A market in one of those towns addressed all of the rural residents' consumer needs with the sign, "Groceries and Firearms." In the harbor at Garibaldi, I saw gulls chasing an eagle from their territory, and farther north, a dense fog bank caused the road in front of me to vanish, forcing me to change course. In Tillamook, where cows far outnumber people, I ate local cheese and lost myself identifying familiar literary adventures painted on a wall in the library.

At a rest stop identified as Winema Wayfinding Point, I stopped to take in the view of the ocean and ponder the term, "wayfinding." More than merely locating your physical position at a moment in time, the word suggests the need to consider one's path. Taking time to appreciate the path I had the privilege to travel, I ate lunch on a sun-warmed stone bench with a commanding view.

The nomadic life can change one's perspective. Just such a shift occurred the night I was feeling put-out when the driver of a ten wheel semi-tractor trailer pulled alongside my riverfront parking spot at a rest stop south of Tillamook. The truck created a wall fourteen-foot-high and fifty-foot long so close to the van that the door on the driver's side couldn't be opened. To make matters worse, the driver did not turn off the vehicle's annoyingly loud engine.

This was not the first time my sleep was disturbed by a noisy truck, and it wouldn't be the last, but this time, my irritation was transformative. After some fussing and fuming, I came to the realization that "you don't own this." Recognizing that I was a temporary guest at this rest stop, in this town, and in this body triggered a shift in consciousness. Gratitude outshined the resentment I was feeling as I moved my vehicle to the other end of the parking lot. We are all just passing through.

Stormy Weather

While dealing with repairs that kept me in Oregon longer than planned, winter rains kicked in. The work on the van was completed at the end of the day on November 30th, leaving me one day to make my date with the Arcata Threshold Choir in Northern California. As excited as I was to resume my quest, I was not eager to say goodbye to Joe. Lately, each time we part, sadness comes over me that feels like a stone weighing heavily on my heart. It would be at least a year before we would see each other again, and moving closer to the end of my time on this earth, I am aware of the possibility that each goodbye could be the last. I feel a similar sadness leaving old friends, and new friends met along the way, not knowing when, or if, I will see them again. That pull at the heartstrings reminds me that each minute spent with the ones we love is precious.

That night in my campsite, I decorated my little cabin with cheery battery-operated string lights while singing "Christmas Don't be Late" in a silly chipmunk voice. Heavy showers pounded the roof all night, but the morning was radiant with starbursts of sunlight reflected in puddles and wet foliage. An unexpected warm wind was a sure sign a storm was moving in as I prepared for a seven-hour drive south on the winding coast highway.

With wheels aligned and new ball joints and wipers, Wanda handled well plowing through powerful cross-winds, even on exposed bridges. After a stop in Coos Bay at the 1950s classic, the Pancake Mill restaurant (I don't care what others think, I get a warm fuzzy feeling when waitresses call me sweetheart), the wind picked up and serious rain began to fall. The viewpoint at Port Orford was my next planned stop, but the wind was so strong, I felt the need to keep my distance from the lookout on the cliff. I can't shake feeling spooked after learning about the woman in Ireland who was blown off a cliff one stormy night while she slept in her "caravan" a few miles from the hostel where I was staying in Dingle.

An hour down the road, I was forced to stop at Gold's Beach to wait out a deluge that delivered raging wind, lightning, thunder, and sideways rain and hail. Taking refuge in a bookstore café for hours, I kept my distance from the plate glass window that shuddered ominously with each powerful blast of wind. Back on the road I leaned on my mantra of "Wonder driven, not fear driven," to face the storm. I discovered that with my water and gas tanks full, and the van fully loaded down with my belongings, the weight carried low in the vehicle acted as a keel, helping me stay the course in winds gusting to forty miles an hour, and higher on exposed bridges.

I had to cancel my plans to join a community singing circle in Arcata that night. Just south of the California border, I stopped to spend the night next to the frog pond at Lagoon Creek Rest Stop. The rest stop is near the Yurok Reservation, and the spot in the Klamath River where a gray whale and her calf were stranded during the summer of 2011. The whales languished in plain sight of the highway for two weeks, and my visit to Joe's that summer required driving through the crowds gathered to see the phenomenon. A carnival-like atmosphere kept me from stopping to join the gawkers on the bridge. Whales are sacred to the Native people of this land, and they offered drumming, flute music, and prayers to help guide them back to the sea.

I made it to Arcata in time for the morning practice. On my sojourns to visit Joe and Gretchen in Oregon over the past fifteen years, Arcata has been a regular stop for family time with my brother and sister-in-law and my nephews, Joaquin and Ruben. This was my first time to meet with the three-year-old Arcata Threshold Choir. With mentoring, dedication, and expert leadership from volunteer coaches, the midwifing of new chapters begun by Kate continues.

This chapter was preparing for a seasonal event for hospice, as were other chapters I visited. The official visitor liaison, Donna, reached out and made me feel welcome. We immediately recognized each other from TCI gatherings, which is always a pleasant surprise. With so many new faces wherever I go, it is comforting to see a face that is familiar.

Arcata's music director, Maggie, is a also a talented community singing circle leader. The choir practiced a mix of Threshold music and songs that were new to me. They opened and closed with upbeat songs, and the entire morning was a joyful experience. As a visitor, I don't know all of the songs that chapters choose to sing. I can join them singing enough songs to feel part of the group, and being introduced to new songs is a always a bonus.

This is where I started taking photos of choirs. For

some reason, I hadn't thought of doing this until Dr. B made the suggestion. The pictures started in Arcata, choir stop number ten on my journey.

In California, signs that say "No Overnight Parking" are posted at every parking lot, rest area, and roadside pull-out. As a "full-timer," I could easily spend $3,000 on campsites each month if I stayed in RV parks every night. Finding places to safely park for free can involve hours of searching neighborhoods for hidden parking lots and abandoned roads, like the stretch of old highway along the Eel River where I parked near the town of Garberville.

Marijuana production supports a large percentage of the population in Humboldt County, California, and for decades, the parking lot of Ray's Food Place in downtown Garberville has been an unofficial "farmers market" for sellers, buyers, and devotees of the prized herb. Perhaps walking through the cloud of skunky smelling smoke to get to the entry of the market had an effect on me. I left the store with a pumpkin pie, cream for whipping, and a small bottle of Jameson's Whiskey.

Having recently finished reading John Steinbeck's *Travels with Charley*, I felt compelled to add whiskey to my provisions for occasions when I might want to entertain, as JS did. In the van's well-stocked pantry, I carried the whisk, pure vanilla extract, and sugar needed to make fresh whipped cream just the way I like it. Parked on the banks of the Eel River under a brilliant sunset sky, I entertained myself that night with an irrational evening meal of pie and hot chocolate with a shot of Jameson's, both heavy on the whipped cream.

Sacred Forests

Diverting off Highway 101 to drive the winding Avenue of the Giants is an immersion into the fragrant shadow world of ancient redwoods. On this glorious morning, sunlight streamed through the treetops, transforming redwood circles into radiant altars.

I once attended a wedding held in just such a forest. Ruthie, the tightrope walker, and Billy, the clown, performers I befriended when their traveling circus passed through Venice Beach in 1973, were married in a ring of old-growth coastal redwoods like these. The bride rode into the sunlit opening in the forest on a white horse with the long train of her wedding dress trailing behind, and her hair and horse bedecked in flowers. Ruthie's attendants, costumed in Renaissance finery, helped her dismount and escorted her to a lacy canopy in the center of the sacred circle of trees where Billy waited. Among the elaborately costumed guests in the dreamlike ceremony, a fantastic satyr goat-man coyly darted in and out of the trees playing a pan flute. Even without magicians and mythical creatures, there is deep magic in redwood forests.

Back on the Highway traveling south toward Sonoma I drove past the Stafford exit, the site of the 1997 Headwaters Forest Protest. I participated in that protest with my sons and 8,000 other tree huggers, including Mickey Hart, Bonnie Raitt, Bob Weir, Graham Nash, and our progressive California Governor, Jerry Brown. Courageous Julia Butterfly would begin her epic tree-sit within sight of this spot two months later.

Beckoned by the ancient forest.

CHAPTER 6

When the
Heart Sings

Although this would be my first opportunity to sing with the Valley of the Moon Threshold Choir chapter in Sonoma, members who are long-time friends from sixteen years living in the area made this stop a warm homecoming. Eleanor, the director, is an environmental activist, educator, and songleader I have long admired. At the practice, her thoughtful approach to ending songs inspired me. Instead of closing her hand, as most choir directors do to signal the end, Eleanor invites the song to continue to resonate, raising her arm with an open hand to send it soaring.

Eleanor reminds us that the songs we sing are meaningful blessings the world desperately needs. Her intention to guide songs to continue resonating is one of the gems I carried with me to share with the choir chapters I visited.

Kate Munger tells us, "The messages contained in the songs we sing guide us to live with compassion and acceptance toward ourselves and others." The official Threshold Choir repertoire currently consists of close to 500 songs offering comfort and support, many written by Kate and other choir members. There are songs written by professional songwriters, most from talent within our midst, and songs by choir members who may have never written a song before they were inspired by this work. "Sending You Light," by Melanie DeMore,[12] "May Peace

Be With You," by Annie Garretson,[13] "Deeply Loved," by Marilyn Power Scott,[14] and "Walking Each Other Home," by Kate Munger are some of the core songs regularly sung by Threshold Choir chapters at bedsides, practices, and gatherings around the world.

When I joined Threshold, the songbook consisted of sheet music for over 350 songs that Kate had lovingly scored by hand with lyrics meticulously written in her schoolteacher cursive. I studied the written music and sang along with learning CDs every day, falling asleep and waking with the music echoing in my head. The gift of those songs continues to recharge my spirit with love and compassion. The music resonates deeply with those of us who have chosen this service, and that connection adds to the sincerity of our singing. Kate says that you know Threshold Choir is your calling if the songs give you a shiver.

Although sheet music helps us learn the songs precisely as the songwriters intended, the *a cappella* singing we do at bedsides is done without written scores. The work we do to commit the songs to heart allows us to sing from the heart. It takes practice to hold your part without sheet music to guide you, especially when singing harmony parts in small bedside ensembles of three or four singers.

Harmonies elevate the melodies we sing, and singing in unison can bring a song home. It is magical to hear a group singing in unison lock in on the same pitch and seamlessly blend their voices. The result can fill the room with the sound of a large choir, or mysteriously meld into one voice with individual voices completely indistinguishable. Landing on that sweet spot can result in a vibration that continues to ring in the room after the singers leave.

On the Threshold Choir website, Ellen Rose offers this description of singing in unison and in harmony:

Singing in unison celebrates our human connection, that we are literally on the same wavelength.

Singing in harmony celebrates our diversity, that out of our differences can come an amazing energy with the power to move ourselves and others.

Song Choices

Trust that songs with the right message will surface at the right time guides song choices at bedsides. The more songs we learn, the better prepared we are to come up with a song that is needed in a particular moment. The pool we draw from is far from static; new songs continue to surface and be added to the Threshold Choir repertoire. In the final months of her life, Lauren Lane Powell, a beloved choir director, songwriter, and voice teacher, contributed dozens of songs that share the grace of her journey towards death. As many who contribute songs to the repertoire tell us, Lauren said the music came through her, not from her.

Information about a patient from hospice personnel, caregivers, death doulas, family members, friends, or the patients themselves, along with the treasured belongings on display in their home or hospital room help us in song choices. Paying close attention to a client's body language and facial expression tell us when to start and stop singing. We sing "letting go" songs only at the very end of life when we know they will be appreciated.

At a bedside where grown children and teenaged

grandchildren filled the room of a hospice patient who was hours from death, our chapter sang the "letting go" songs we reserve for the actively dying. While we sang "From My Heart to Yours," a tissue box was passed around the room as one by one, each family member opened to the emotions they were feeling, letting tears flow. We were taking our leave when a family member thanked us for the words they had not been able to bring themselves to say. Sung softly and gently, the message of that song broke them open, freeing them from what they believed was their "duty" to stay strong for the dying family member, and each other. The song was a catalyst for genuine feelings to be shared.

From My Heart to Yours
©2004 by Maria Culberson

From my heart to yours, a song without end.
May it offer you comfort and healing my friend.
Though I cannot go with you, your journey goes on.
I can laugh with you, cry with you, sing till you've won
your freedom from suffering, released from all fear.
May you find all the love that you needed is here.

Most bedside songs are short and uncomplicated, requiring little effort to follow on the part of the listener. Singing simple songs in repetition is a proven formula for reducing pain and anxiety. Threshold Choir singers sometimes drop the words entirely, and hum, or sing "oo" to the melody when the moment calls for pure soothing sound. When our lullaby singing eases patients to sleep, we sometimes sing to their dreams.

On one hospice sing, the Threshold Choir of Pacific Grove entered a hospital room to find the patient was agitated, yelling, and pulling at her intravenous line trying to get out of bed. After summoning nurses, and moving out of the way to give the staff room to help the distressed woman, we noticed the patient who shared the room was cowering under her covers, nervously clutching a teddy bear. She looked as frightened as a child in a thunderstorm when we offered to sing for her.

As the disturbance continued at the other end of the room, singing "We Call This Place Into Peace," "Breathe Easy," and "May Only Love Surround You," and humming, had a calming effect. Even in the midst of the commotion, offering what Melanie DeMore has called, "An IV of caring," brought peace to the anxious roommate. She was drifting off to sleep when we left her bedside.

Choosing what to sing to a patient at any particular moment in time can be challenging. Even with careful observation, training, and years of bedside singing experience, we may not always be able to tune into a patient's needs or desires in the moment.

On one hospice visit, our choir was surprised by a patient's emotional response to our singing. Tender songs like "Metta Sutta" and "Sweet, Sweet, Dreams," moved Millie to tears and sadness that grew with alarming intensity. Between heaving sobs she told us, "It is all too sad!" For many of us, accepting the gift of compassion, something Jack Kornfield describes as "the meeting of love and pain," [15] can bring to the surface the vulnerability and need we may be masking. On our next visit, intending to sing only "happy songs," we found Millie in a different mood. This time she was all smiles. She surprised us by singing along to "Sending You Light," a song she heard for the first time during our previous visit.

One long-time choir member shared an experience that her choir had singing Melanie DeMore's, "Lead With Love," in response to a request for a lively song. The patient was all in, visibly taken by the song's catchy rhythm and inspiring message of hope with its repeating chorus; *"Put one foot in front of the other and lead with love,"* and the refrain, *"One foot, one foot, one foot."* Seeing the patient's prosthetic leg as they left the room, the singers were taken aback when they realized they had been singing to an amputee with only one foot. The irony of the circumstance did not interfere with the pleasure, and likely, amusement, it provided the patient.

Requests

Sometimes, patients are not interested in the comforting Threshold Choir music and intricate harmonies we work so hard to perfect. In Aromas, California, choir members spent many months singing to a cancer patient who only wanted to hear Doris Day tunes. Playful Wendy Collura told me of singing the kid's song, "B-I-N-G-O," at a bedside with the Threshold Choir of Cleveland, Ohio, after being asked to wait for the patient's family to return from playing bingo in the facility's recreation room. When all had gathered around the bedside, the entire family happily joined in when Wendy started the sing with that familiar song.

Another story from Cleveland revealed the power of a song requested for a memorial service. Asked if they could sing "Holy Angels," a song by Sara Thomsen that the mother had sung every evening to her son who passed after a long illness, the choir practiced until they were confident they had it. While singing the requested song at the memorial, Wendy said there was a moment when "everything and everyone in the room came together." She was certain the departed son was with them.

Familiar songs can be meaningful and uplifting. My local Trader Joe's market gets this, shopping to the groove of Motown, the Beatles, and funk, I am a happy shopper in no hurry to leave. Songs from the past can provide support and an opportunity for connection for patients who suffer from Alzheimer's and dementia, as documented in the amazing film, *Alive Inside*.[16]

Cynthia Dyer, the director of the Long Bay Threshold Singers of North Carolina, told me of the confused look that she noticed on the face of a hospice patient they sang to in a memory care unit. Hearing the patient singing to herself, "I don't care if I never come back," from "Take Me Out to the Ballgame," Cynthia understood that the woman wanted to hear songs that she knew. Switching to "Americana" songs from the patient's childhood relaxed her and brought a smile to her face. For Cynthia, this was a lesson that some patients, "want something familiar to hang on to, something that helps them remember who they are."

The Pacific Grove chapter had the privilege to sing with Dan twice a month over a period of 18 months before we were called to his bedside in his final hours. I say "sing with" instead of "sing to," because Dan only wanted to hear songs that gave him an opportunity to sing along.

Our first visit came as the result of a friend telling me her husband was gravely ill and passing long miserable hours staring out the hospital window singing, "Don't Fence Me In." We learned the Western classic to sing with him, intending to spend most of our first visit comforting him with the compassionate Threshold Choir songs we had so diligently practiced. As frail as Dan was, he perked up hearing his song, and with a strained, raspy voice, joined us in the choruses. His disquiet and drumming fingers signaled that he had no patience for our sweet Threshold songs; he did not want to be soothed.

Seeing how the singing lifted his spirit, we agreed that we would comply with Dan's request to sing songs familiar to him on our regular visits. Many chapters I visited around the country choose to leave sing-alongs to other musicians, maintaining a tranquil sacred tone at bedsides by singing only Threshold Choir repertoire. Our visits with Dan were far from that. His son, a frequent visitor, began giving him DVDs of Broadway musicals when he saw how the music lifted his father's mood.

When Dan left the hospital to spend his remaining months at home, watching those musicals was his main pastime. During our visits, he wanted to sing that music with us. "Surrey with the Fringe on Top," "Oh, What a Beautiful Morning," and "Bali Ha'i" transported him back to a happier time in his life. Our songbooks swelled with music for the show tunes we learned to sing with Dan, and he scolded if we tried to add our own harmonies. To honor his illustrious career diving for jade off the coast of Big Sur, we collaborated on lyrics to a song celebrating his adventures that we sang to the tune of

"Michael Row Your Boat Ashore." Dan's contribution to the lyrics speak to his colorful life:

Grab the gear and get a net, Alleluia,
We get our jade with work and sweat, Alleluia.
Body is aching and the back is stiff, Alleluia,
Warm beer waiting at the top of the cliff, Alleluia.

Dan was at home, lying in his hospital bed with labored breathing and eyes closed, when we were asked to come for a final visit. His adoring wife lay beside him for most of the ninety minutes that we softly sang a mix of Threshold Choir songs, his favorite tunes, and the song we had written together. He was unresponsive, but with the understanding that hearing is the last sense to go, we continued what we hoped would be a comforting send-off for his journey.

I signaled to Suzan and Jill when I thought it was time to sing the spiritual, "Swing Low Sweet Chariot," a song that so often elicited responses from those we sang to. Under the covers, we could see Dan's toes begin to keep time to the music, and then his hands moved rhythmically, ever so slightly. As we continued singing the familiar song, he opened his eyes, looked at his wife, and whispered, "I love you," before returning to the unresponsive state that would continue until he passed three hours later. We were pleased by this confirmation that the offering of songs was reaching him, and touched by his tender goodbye to his wife.

As time passed, a deeper understanding about being an impartial witness at bedsides led me to view the deathbed experience with Dan through a different lens. I have come to the realization that familiar songs, with the power to break through very real communication barriers, may be a disruption for the actively dying. Songs that anchor us to memories and loved ones may tether us to the life we are in the process of leaving behind, interfering with the work of detachment that is a part of the death process. If our candle is slowly burning out at the time of death, familiar songs may fan the flame. Ethereal Threshold Choir songs are meant to gently wash over a patient, flowing with the river that is their journey in progress.

I don't want to judge the song choice that elicited a response during Dan's final hours by the standards of right and wrong. Saying goodbye to his beloved may have been exactly what Dan needed at that moment to enable him to continue his process of letting go of the life he had clung to so tenaciously. What I learned from that remarkable bedside experience has helped me more clearly define my role as a bedside singer. A demonstration of the power of song, the experience helped me better comprehend the responsibilities that come of being invited to a bedside to bring a humble offering of song.

Cynthia Dyer told of the clarity that came to her at the deathbed of a hospice patient the Long Bay Threshold Singers had sung to for two years. With the patient in decline, the family asked her to come alone; they were not feeling up to a group visit. Noticing Miss D's breathing was slow and that her eyes were half closed, Cynthia sensed death was near. On previous visits, Miss D had requested favorite hymns that she loved to sing with the choir members who came to her bedside. Choosing not to sing those hymns, Cynthia intuitively knew, "this was the time to sing music that wasn't familiar. I didn't want to pull her back. I didn't want to give her the responsibility of being the audience, feeling a need to respond or thank me in some way."

Cynthia recognized the advantage of softly singing Threshold Choir repertoire that would not give the patient a familiar hook to hold on to. With the patient in the process of crossing over, Cynthia chose "letting go" songs to support her journey. She remembers singing "Pure Grace," and feeling compelled to softly repeat the last words of the verses, "let go," over and over until she saw that Miss D had let go of her body and was no longer breathing.

Followed by Vultures.

CHAPTER 7

You Are Not Alone

Lingering in Glen Ellen, I spent time with friends I consider family, sang with Threshold Choirs in the area and answered my heart's call to return to the northern California coast.

Where the Pacific Coast Highway bravely clings to the edge of the coastal mountains north of the Russian River, I couldn't help noticing vultures were following. Riding the updrafts, sitting on fence posts, and swooping perilously close to the windshield in front of my moving vehicle, it was clear they were watching me. A hike on a tawny mountainside overlooking the sea brought them closer.

Being followed by vultures feels ominous despite those magnificent wings that shine as pure and white as angel's wings in the sunlight. In the poem "Vulture," Robinson Jeffers writes of lying very still on the ground to tempt a vulture to circle closer, and laments that it is not yet his time. He ends the poem with these lines: "To be eaten by that beak and become part of him, to share those wings and those eyes — What a sublime end of one's body, what an enskyment; What life after death."[17] I am not that brave.

Camping in an enchanted pocket of redwood forest on the Gualala River, a forest ranger collecting camp fees had a questionnaire to complete. She was charged with documenting camper's home zip code, which I didn't have; how long I would stay, which I couldn't say; and what direction I was headed, which I wasn't sure.

When she asked about my adventure, to explain the trip and Threshold Choir, I shared one of the songs, "You Are Not Alone," by Kate Munger.

I am not timid about singing to strangers given the opportunity. A song is a simple gift, a gift I can give. I find that I often have a song that a moment calls for, and I'm not shy about piping in with, "I've got a song for that." My intention is not performance, and knowing that no one is going to be wowed by my humble voice puts the focus on the message, not on me. Spontaneous song feels playful. In Hawaii there is a common expression that I enthusiastically embrace, "No shame."

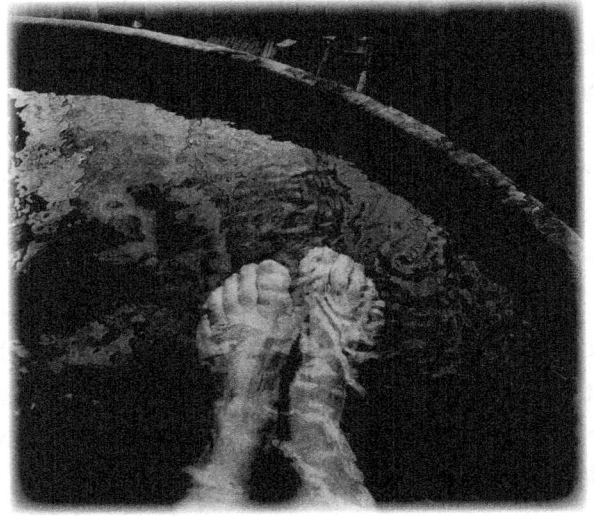

Ahh!

Two hours north of Gualala, charming Mendocino is a place I have often visited over the years with my kayak lashed to the top of my little Toyota and my tent packed in the trunk. I spent many peaceful hours there paddling upstream to the headwaters of Little River where the dense forest prevents further passage. After walking the magnificent Mendocino headlands, a soak in a redwood hot tub at the Sweetwater Inn, and berry cobbler at the Mendocino Hotel, I continued north to the tiny town of Casper to find a place to park for the night.

I was sound asleep when an angry voice approaching the van awakened me. With the doors locked and curtains closed, I felt safe inside, but I was uncertain what this intruder might do to the outside of the van. Listening for footsteps, I heard nothing more. Not battened down enough to drive away, and concerned that turning on lights could escalate the situation, the disturbance prompted me to secure my belongings in the dark. With everything in place, and hearing no further commotion, I laid down with keys in hand, ready to drive away if the situation called for action.

I slept for another hour before hearing the loud, aggressive voice again. I can only guess that this was a person camped in the bushes nearby who did not want me parking so close. Ready this time, I moved the van a few blocks and parked in front of the church in one-block downtown Casper, where I felt safe. The experience taught me a valuable lesson. From that point on, I would make sure the van was ready to drive away before I went to sleep. The ability to move from the bed to the driver's seat without exiting the vehicle is a safety feature I fully appreciate.

Returning to wine country, I joined a practice of the Napa Valley Threshold Choir. Sudie, the director of the choir, made me feel like a treasured guest with her kindness and interest in my journey. She organized a welcoming potluck dinner prior to the practice. There were gifts, original bedside songs written by chapter members, and sweet little paintings of singing angels that Echo gave to each of us. I answered questions about the trip and taught the song that moved me to claim my wild self, retire from my nonprofit work, and leave my home in Pacific Grove, "I'm a Wild One Now." Sudie sent me off with CDs of bedside songs written by the members of this chapter with the request that I distribute them to choirs I visit.

Waking in Sudie's driveway with a brightly colored hot air balloon overhead was the perfect start for a lovely Wine Country day. I drove back to Sonoma Valley to join members of the Valley of the Moon and Sonoma County Threshold Singers honoring the coming winter solstice. We met in Angela's home for the songfest. She was my neighbor in this cul-de-sac where Kel and I lived when we moved from Maui in 1989, and her house is across the street from the driveway that Ritch and Margie made available for my stay in Glen Ellen. A shared commitment to this service has enriched friendships I had with choir members like Angela before any of us joined Threshold Choir. Eleanor provided copies of the solstice songs we sang, explaining that some were from the rounds-singing group that Kate Munger started before she founded Threshold Choir.

Returning to Pacific Grove, I met with my home choir and shared songs and techniques gleaned from chapters I had visited. We also joined friends from the Wholehearted Chorus tribe for a winter solstice bonfire on Asilomar Beach that happened to fall on a spectacular full moon night. A song I learned from the Portland chapter, "When Soul Meets Winter," was added to the offering of songs, poems, prayers, and blessings honoring seasonal change that is shared at those rituals. For many years, friends have gathered around a blazing fire on this beach for solstice ceremonies and for Threshold Choir practices. The tradition of coming together to sing around a fire at the edge of grandmother ocean renews our connection to each other, the elements, and the ancestors.

Spending the holidays with family was good for my soul. Kel prepared a holiday feast, my granddaughter, Ashley, honored family tradition with a gingerbread house, and my great-grandson, Vinny, took on the task of smashing and eating the confection on Christmas Day, a job once delegated to my sons. All was well in my world.

I closed the year singing with members of the Santa Cruz Threshold Singers in a conference room at a public library. Invited to park in a member's driveway, I was just steps away from the water's edge where surfers challenged the heaving winter waves on tiny surfboards. Shondeya and I dove into deep conversation over a breakfast of sunny papayas seasoned with lime juice. She spoke of how important Threshold Choir is to her wellbeing, offering an opportunity to provide meaningful service, and a supportive family. We agreed the choir gives our lives purpose.

A Difficult Decision

Leaving Santa Cruz, I chose to spend a night in the magnificent redwoods of the Santa Cruz mountains on the way to Oakland, and New Year's Day with my son.

Siri's directions led me to an impossibly rough mountain road with potholes, steep climbs, hairpin turns, downhill stretches that made my brakes smoke, and no place to turn around. By the time I found a suitable place to pull off the road for the night, the awful wheel squeal that developed on Bainbridge Island was back, and I was far from any repair shops at the onset of a four-day New Year's holiday weekend.

After a fitful night, things looked brighter in the morning with the metal-on-metal scraping occurring only at sharp turns. After preparing coffee and breakfast in a lovely park, I headed back to Oakland to wait for repair shops to reopen after the long holiday weekend. I often stayed in Oakland with Kel. He would spend days creating feasts for the two of us, preparing elegant meals with only the freshest local ingredients. He once made my favorite hibiscus tea, jamaica, poured over ice cubes in which he had frozen sliced kumquats. As an artist and a foodie, he loves the diversity Oakland offers, and he has helped me grow to appreciate the vibrant culture, politics, music, art, and the diversity of ethnic food offerings to be found there.

Kind Kel has encouraged me in every aspect of my journey and my writing. He even found a way for me to camp within the padlocked gates of his backyard, safe from the break-ins and car thefts that commonly occur on the streets in his neighborhood. To maneuver into and out of his backyard, I needed his assistance to navigate the narrow alley and open the heavy gates, a task which sometimes requires removing the trash and furniture that accumulates in the alley overnight. Because he was leaving town a day before repair shops would reopen, I would need to find another place to overnight in Oakland while I waited.

With hundreds of parked cars and RVs sheltering people living on the streets just blocks from Kel's apartment, it would have been easy to find a spot to park for the night without getting a ticket for illegally sleeping in my vehicle. At least 4,000 people lived on the streets of Oakland during the winter of 2018/2019; it is many times that now. The presence of encampments at busy intersections, on roadway medians, and alongside Oakland's highways makes it impossible to ignore the struggle for survival so many of our neighbors face every day. The shelter vehicles provide for the unhoused does not lessen the hardship of living without running water, sanitation, or the ability to dispose of the trash that accumulates in mounds around vehicles and encampments. As if that isn't enough to endure, residents of these vehicles and camps live with the constant threat that their shelters will be targeted by city bulldozers in the periodic clearings that leave them with nowhere to go.

I was not facing those hardships. I was living the dream with a toilet, a heater, hot and cold running water, and the ability to travel freely. I felt my privilege would make me an intruder on the streets, resented, and very possibly, a target for theft. I chose to stay in a hotel that night, using credit card points I was accumulating with each gas purchase.

I am still troubled by that choice. I may have missed an opportunity to abandon the notion that I'm different than people who are living in vehicles on the streets of

Oakland. After dedicating so many years working to house the unhoused in Monterey County, the irony of the situation is not lost on me.

The Fruitvale auto shop where Wanda would be repaired is located in the Oakland Coliseum neighborhood near the infamous Fruitvale BART station. With scores of Mexican restaurants, Aztec murals and street vendors selling tacos, tamales, and freshly squeezed orange juice under brightly colored umbrellas, this colorful part of town feels like another country.

While the repair was underway, I waited in the office where the shop owner attended to paperwork and phone calls. He changed the Spanish language TV channel to an English station for me, and when a newscaster spoke of progress on the border wall with Mexico, I asked what he thinks about Trump's wall. He told me his story of being wrongly deported to Mexico, explaining that in the custody of ICE he did not have the right to make a phone call to his family or an attorney. He said that he was legally living in the US at the time of his deportation and owned a home and business here. It took him six years, three attorneys, and thousands of dollars to get back into the US. He also told me he was a Trump supporter. He saw President Trump as a "good businessman," something he greatly admired.

Invited to join the Threshold Singers of the East Bay in Oakland for an afternoon practice, I worked with other members to learn one of Lauren Lane Powell's songs, "Flowing Free." The director, Sherrin, led the group on Skype because she had a cold that she didn't want to spread, unknowingly previewing what was to come with COVID-19 Zoom singing. A recording of the song reached Lauren in her last two weeks of life. Lauren was very public about her bouts with cancer, and she shared her approach to infusing chemotherapy treatments with hope and gratitude using song.[18]

Traveling around the Bay Area, I met with three other Threshold Choirs. I spent a night in Morgan Hill, where Katie, who had been a member of the Aromas Threshold Choir, graciously hosted me. Katie and her husband, Rusty, may be the kindest people I have ever known, and Katie's lovable service dog, Gelsey, is nothing short of a miracle. Trained as a dog for diabetic service, Gelsey performed the life-saving task of loving Katie up to alert her when her blood sugar dropped. During one of our practices, Gelsey was unrelenting with her kisses, even though Katie's blood sugar tested at acceptable levels. When Katie asked if there was someone else in the room with diabetes who may be experiencing a drop in blood sugar, we learned that Gelsey had sensed Sreya's blood sugar drop from across the room.

It had been about six years since I visited Katie and Rusty at their ranch-like refuge that backs up to a creek and the rugged mountains that separate California's inland valleys from the coast. When I trained with the Aromas Choir, another Threshold Choir singer, Amrita, lived in the guest house that now serves as an art studio.

After dinner, Katie invited me inside the candlelit sanctuary to cull through pictures cut from magazines to create a Soul Collage, a Tarot-style image of intentions for my journey. Rumi holding a flute in a golden forest emerged. Katie played her crystal bowls for me before

I wandered back to my van for what was possibly the best night's sleep of the entire expedition. I would return a week later for a reunion with the Aromas chapter.

The Gas Station of Shame

I arrived in San Francisco three hours before the practice of the spectacular San Francisco Threshold Choir, giving myself time to walk to Golden Gate Park. With the song "San Francisco" (Be Sure to Wear Flowers in Your Hair) spinning in my head, I took my time savoring the experience of Haight Street on the way to the park. It was little changed since the Summer of Love.

The smell of patchouli oil and pot still hangs in the air, store windows still display the bell bottoms, scant crocheted tops, and the paisley we wore in the Sixties, groups of wild-child teens still hang out at the corner of Haight and Ashbury Streets, and I even passed kids listening to Van Morrison tunes on a boom box. Some of the same businesses remained after fifty years, one exception being the Whole Foods market that occupies the corner of Haight and Stanyon Streets where the "Gas Station of Shame" once stood.

It was 1969 when my hippie husband and I stopped at that Union 76 station to fill the gas tank of the panel truck that was our home. While we were busy at the pump, our dog, Lucille, hopped out of the truck, and because she was in heat, she was soon in the company of a male dog taking full advantage of the situation. The dogs got hung up, and crying in terror (or was it pain?) they tried to untangle their interlocked genitals by running in the opposite directions. Screaming obscenities at

Phil and me, the gas station owner ordered us to put a stop to the vulgar display. Pitiful Lucille looked to us to rescue her, but having never witnessed such a debacle, we had no idea what to do. The irate proprietor ended the calamity by spraying the dogs with a hose, freeing them from their entanglement with a shock of cold water.

Then came the pipe wrench bargaining. We had no money to pay for the gas, and Phil, a mechanic who carried a large wooden treasure box filled with tools, handed the proprietor a rusty wrench in payment. This system of barter was not appreciated by businesses, but Phil, who was convinced that money was the source of all evil, was committed to it. In those days, when you pumped first and paid later, or in the case of the Golden Gate Bridge, paid after crossing, it was possible to pull off such an exchange. How this payment arrangement never resulted in police involvement is a mystery.

The San Francisco Threshold Choir is large. On the evening I joined them, forty singers came together to practice in a church hall a block from Haight Street. Many were familiar from years of gatherings. During the the practice, rotating songleaders took time to stop and review pitches and timing for each song. Special events help fuel the high energy of this chapter; they had just completed their annual New Year's Day sing at Golden Gate Park, and were preparing for the annual hospice "Night of Remembrance," and an upcoming leadership council retreat.

Palo Alto, a lush sanctuary nestled in the hills half-an-hour south of San Francisco, is the home of the Peninsula Threshold Choir. Reconnecting with Ellen was a delight. She is someone I deeply admire for her long-standing commitment to the choir that included serving as the webmaster for many years. As a new choir director, I peppered her with questions and could always count on her lightning quick responses to be the guidance I needed. Cathy, one of the co-directors of the chapter, would become a cherished supporter of my journey, regularly following my blog and sending gas donations.

The choir sang "Duerme" to me, the one and only song I have contributed to the Threshold Choir repertoire. They also shared bedside songs their members have written. I was offered a songbath in a reclining chair placed in the center of the circle. As I received the gift, I was able to fully appreciate this choir's mastery of blending voices to sound like one voice.

From the beginning, Kate encouraged each choir to give each other the gift of receiving song in a reclining "Zero Gravity" chair when we come together to rehearse. The recipient in the chair may be asked if they have any song requests, but other than that, there is no talking during a songbath. Singers are fully present for the person receiving chair time, with all of the compassion, reverence, and silence between songs that is offered at a bedside.

For the person in the chair, the experience provides an opportunity to momentarily surrender the burdens, sorrows, fears, and the defenses that we carry. Kate describes what we feel surrounded by gentle song as "floating, clouds and comfort." The chair gives us practice being comfortable giving and receiving the gift, and a chance to experience the vulnerability felt by the people we sing to at bedsides. For those of us who are used to being in the driver's seat, and that would be me, receiving song in the chair is a trust fall into loving arms. There are often tears.

A Great Loss

It was bittersweet to return to the tiny, one stop sign village of Aromas to sing with the Threshold Choir angels who took me under their wings. Five of us gathered in Linda's kitchen where a potluck meal and Linda's birthday celebration preceded the singing. I had seen Joan, Linda, and Katie at choir gatherings over the years, but too much time had passed since we had gathered to sing together like this. I missed these amazing women and our weekly sings.

After another sweet night at Katie and Rusty's, we said goodbye the next morning. Sadly, this would be my last visit with dear Katie, I learned that she had passed in her sleep a year after our visit. Rumi's words eloquently speak to Katie's legacy, "Your acts of kindness are iridescent wings of divine love which linger & continue to uplift others long after your sharing."

Lisa G. Littlebird, Spreading Wholehearted Chorus Joy.

CHAPTER 8

Vitamin Sing

I stretched my stay on the Monterey Peninsula by a few weeks to attend the January 2019 Littlebird Songleader Flight School Retreat in Carmel Valley. The reunion with Lisa G Littlebird, songleaders from her online courses, and friends from Wholehearted Chorus for days of singing together at the Songleader Retreat provided a blast of what Lisa calls "vitamin sing." We bonded learning songs, taking turns leading, and participating in playful activities like team songwriting.

Joining Lisa's community singing tribe in 2014 opened the door to a parallel universe, a singing revolution fueled by socially conscious songs that encourage love and gratitude for each other, the earth, and all beings. No audition is required, all are invited to join the circle. In the chorus, each and every participant receives support and encouragement from Lisa and the other members of the group. As word of the uplifting weekly gatherings and seasonal concerts spread, Lisa's circles in Big Sur and Monterey swelled to 160 singers by 2018.

After leading singing circles for more than a decade, the recognition that leaders were needed to facilitate the growth of the community singing movement led Lisa to create the online Littlebird Songleader Flight School "in service to our collective healing and upliftment." The courses offer instruction in music theory, organizing a song library, songwriting, voice, breathing, and leading groups with generosity and love. Lisa's Flight School has empowered hundreds of songleaders to start oral tradition community singing circles in their hometowns and cities around the world.

A skilled and generous networker, Lisa invites talented songleaders from near and far to share their music at weekly circles, retreats, and in Flight School offerings. Before I left town in August of 2018, Lisa's singing circles had provided opportunities to sing with Laurence Cole,[19] MaMuse,[20] Heather Houston,[21] Barbara McAfee,[22] Debbie Nargi Brown,[23] Glen Phillips,[24] Marilyn Power Scott,[25] Vernon Bush,[26] Kate Munger, and many others. Melanie DeMore was invited to be a presenter and mentor to her flock after I left on my Threshold Choir tour. With COVID-19, Lisa's Zoom singing parties reached a larger audience with songwriters and singers from around the globe participating.

The circles grow richer as each talented songster adds their own unique voice and character to the collective gumbo. Kate Munger's ritual of holding a moment of sacred stillness after songs and Laurence Cole's layered songs are contributions that have been embraced by the movement and carried forward to singing communities everywhere.

I Feel Better

Spontaneous exclamations of, "I feel better," with arms uplifted may erupt at any time in Lisa G's singing circles. The focus required when we sing may be one of the reasons it is such a blissful exercise. Singing demands that we give our full attention to the present moment. Eckhart Tolle teaches it is impossible to entertain thoughts and be fully present at the same time. When we are singing together, we are one with the music and each other.

Pacia Platzek shared how Lisa's Wholehearted Chorus provided the medicine she needed following her son's sudden death. For months, she sat in the back of the room at practices alternately singing and crying. The songs touched her heart, some bringing an onslaught of tears, while others gave her strength. She said she felt free to let the tears fall with chorus members around her offering their support.

The encouraging and generous focus Lisa shines on each singer in the circle made Pacia feel safe, "Lisa is not looking for something for herself, she strives to fill everyone's cup." While immersed in grief, Pacia found purpose and belonging participating in a Wholehearted Chorus season and concert. When her adoring husband, Gary, saw Pacia's face light up as she performed, he was astounded to witness her happiness at a time when she was dealing with such devastating loss. He encouraged her to keep singing.

Pacia did continue to sing in the chorus. She enrolled in Songleader Flight School and started a number of singing circles in her neighborhood. She also contributed earnings from her art to fund scholarships for those who needed financial help to join Wholehearted Chorus and participate in the Flight School and retreats. Pacia is also a member of the Threshold Choir of Pacific Grove.

Kate's belief that solutions appear as need surfaces may explain the phenomenal rise of choirs and community singing that is bringing people together when unity is so desperately needed. A 2019 Chorus Impact Study showed more than fifty million Americans were singing in choruses. It also revealed that people who sing feel more connected to others, less isolated, and that singers over sixty-five had improved health due to singing.[27]

Melanie DeMore attributes the tremendous increase in the number of community choirs to "the hunger for connection we share." After the extended time-out we endured with COVID-19, and the awareness of our need for connection that was amplified by that isolation, I expect that singing in community will be even more appealing when the the disease is no longer a threat.

A Primal Urge

According to John Blacking, the good feelings we experience when we sing together may be inherited from our prehistoric ancestors. In *How Musical is Man?* he suggests that coming together for ritual singing promoted the cooperation and group cohesiveness our forebearers needed to develop for survival.[28] He believes the euphoric feelings that are the result of singing together may be an instinctive reward that encourages cooperation. Addressing art, evolution, and survival in humans in the book, *On the Origin of Stories: Evolution, Cognition, and Fiction*, Brian Boyd points to the synchronized feeling, movement and "emotional attunement" achieved through human music and dance that gave our ancestors a competitive advantage.[29] The desire to sing together "is in our DNA" according to Melanie DeMore.

Historically, singing in community has been utilized by humans in worship, to share our stories and history, to celebrate, and to grieve. Mothers instinctively sing to babies to show their love and provide comfort. Singing to the sick and dying is another time-honored tradition. Chanting, melodic prayer and sacred music have been a vital part of spiritual and religious practices for millennia. Song and ceremony are inseparably linked.

In his book, *Why Do People Sing?* Paddy Scannell puts forth a theory that humans sing for no other reason than to express emotions.[30] He explains that song touches our hearts and opens us in a way that speaking cannot. Even when singing songs that communicate despair and heartbreak, recognizing that others share those feelings eases isolation and sadness. Songs invite a collective dive into the depth of human experience. We are comforted by the knowledge that we are not alone.

In *Braiding Sweetgrass,* Robin Wall Kimmerer gives an example of the power of song to communicate the feelings that words may not be adequate to express. Hearing her pre-med biology students spontaneously begin singing "Amazing Grace" while on a fieldtrip in the woods was her assurance they had been moved by the wonders of the natural world well beyond the limits of the scientific study of genus and species.[31]

The Power of Song

Laurence Cole, a beloved wizardly elder in the community singing movement, inspires followers of all ages with songs and stories that speak to our need for harmony and playfulness, and to express our grief in these trying times. "Songs for calling up our passion and love, courage and tenderness, joy and reverence for the beauty and grace of life," is how Laurence describes the songs on his CD,

This Fire, which he has made available at no cost on his website, along with his other songs.

Melanie DeMore, the gifted vocal activist and teacher of traditional African rhythms and culture, wrote many of the tender songs of devotion we sing at bedsides. She shares how influential song has been bringing people together, now and throughout history, and explains how song medicine in the form of spirituals provided support and hidden escape messages for enslaved people. She also tells us how rhythm and song provided strength for workers on prison chain gangs. Singing helped activists stay with it when they didn't think they could continue during the civil rights and anti-apartheid movements. Melanie says "We nourish ourselves with song, and from songs, we draw what we need." She promotes singing as the quickest way to bring people together and make them feel part of something bigger than themselves.

Woody Gutherie knew this. The American Folk Music Revival of the 1940s, and Guthrie's recording, *Dust Bowl Ballads,* offered songs that were relevant to the people. Making use of catchy tunes, many already familiar to his audience, topical songs like, "So Long, It's Been Good to Know You," spoke to the struggles of common folk and invited them to sing along. Drawing from the oral tradition of people from Africa and other indigenous cultures, these songs were inclusive and accessible; singing along did not require the ability to read music or play an instrument. The power of song to bring people together in a united front against oppression inspired Woody Guthrie, Pete Seeger, and other singer activists to offer their support for the labor movement of the 1940s.

That power nurtured unity, social change, and the rise of songs supporting the political action of the 1960s. As demands for civil rights grew, music was "the soul of the movement," according to Martin Luther King.[32] Song empowered marchers.

The hymn, "I'll Overcome Someday," was revised to become "We Shall Overcome," one of many anthems of determination civil rights activists adopted. Spirituals like, "Hold On," "This Little Light of Mine," and "We Shall Not Be Moved," took on new meaning, according to Dr. Bernice Johnson Reagon, one of the founders of the Student Nonviolent Coordinating Committee (SNCC) Freedom Singers, and later, Sweet Honey in the Rock. She said the songs gave courage, strength, and hope to freedom marchers,[3]and described protesters singing "as they were dragged into the streets."

John Lewis, who was severely beaten marching for voting rights on "Bloody Sunday," told how demonstrators continued to stand and sing while being beaten by police and jailed.[34]

Ripe with political turmoil, the turbulent 1960s saw music fuel another wave of activist singer-songwriters in support of the rising tide of condemnation for the Vietnam War and the mandatory draft. Folk singers Joan Baez, Bob Dylan, Phil Ochs, and Arlo Guthrie joined Pete Seeger bringing the movement to the people, as did popular rock musicians Richie Havens, Country Joe and the Fish, Credence Clearwater Revival and John Lennon.

Songs that spoke to the concerns of my generation united us in our cause and helped us become a cohesive force for change. At a Joan Baez concert, I saw how the music empowered young men to burn their draft cards, willing to face the legal consequences rather than fight in a war they believed to be wrong.

Alliances with musicians helped Caesar Chavez unite farmworkers. Singing songs like the Mexican folk song, "De Colores," lifted the spirits of strikers enduring the hardships of the 1965 United Farm Workers Union strike. In the 1970s and 1980s, Disco anthems fueled Gay Pride and LGBT activism in the fight for equal rights and an end to the violence directed at that community. "Dolly Parton's "9 to 5" gave traction to the movement for equal pay and an end to the sexual harassment of women in the workplace.

Song continues to energize the fight against oppression. From the encampments of the Occupy Movement to Black Lives Matter marches, music supports social and racial justice movements with songs that speak to the world we want to manifest, and to the rage and trauma fed by injustice. Her's tribute to George Floyd, "I Can't Breathe," winning the award for *Song of the Year* at the 2021 Grammys is validation of song's powerful reach. The songs that touch our hearts are passed down to teach, inspire, and support future generations. They serve as our oral history.

As recognition grows for the need to change deep-rooted racial and social inequities in our society, song helps unite us in that quest. The fact that sports events, including the Super Bowl, are opening with the song known as the Black National Anthem, "Lift Every Voice and Sing," in addition to the traditional "Star-Spangled Banner," gives me hope we are making progress.

Singing Together

Pete Seeger said that "singing together gives people some kind of a holy feeling."[35] The sanctuary of our singing groups offers companionship and a temporary escape from our burdens. Singing together carries us beyond passive listening to the participatory tradition of joining together to make a joyful noise.

Whether performing what Stacy Horn has called "the greatest music humanity has ever produced" in a revered choral group like the one she describes in, *Imperfect Harmony, Finding Harmony Singing With Others,*[36] or singing simple melodies *a cappella* in a trio at bedsides, the effort requires commitment. Singing with others in choirs, choruses, and informal singing circles, we are part of a team. We show up, do the work required to learn the material, and add our voices to create a whole greater than the sum of its parts. It is a tribal experience.

It was in folk singing circles in the late 1960s that I first encountered the heartfelt connection that comes of singing with others. Bonding with those singing with me in every choir and singing group I have participated in since, I have come to realize that the level of connection I feel with the music, rhythm, intention, and the leadership of the group feeds that bond. Singing with others generates an affinity that rarely manifests in other aspects of my life. Lyndsey Scott[37] described singing together as "water for the thirstiest parts of our beings."

The Vulnerability Bond

It is my belief that shared vulnerability among those of us who sing together brings us closer. I learned a lot about this in a college solo performance class, an experience akin to the nightmare of finding oneself naked in a crowd. Students were asked to study four songs each semester, and sing them in front of the class until we got them right while the teacher and students critiqued each pass at the song. The understanding that harsh criticism of someone's singing can wound so deeply that many people spend an entire lifetime without knowing the joy of singing out loud, we learned to support each other's efforts in a positive and compassionate manner. The risks we took singing in front of each other, mistakes and all, and the closeness that developed in the group as a result of those experiences, gave rise to meaningful life-long friendships.

Unlike performers who invest time perfecting a song in private to reduce the risk of making mistakes in front of an audience, participating side by side in chorus and singing circles, we are heard as we learn. Vernon Bush, director of the Glide Ensemble gospel choir and founder of Voice Church, says our authentic voice, the voice he guides singers to access, comes from the belly, the depth of our vulnerability, like the wail of a baby. The image of a puppy lying on its back, intentionally offering its soft belly, suggests the degree of exposure and trust nurtured by singing in community.

Group Mind Connection

It doesn't matter if Kate Munger is introducing a song to a group of 30 or 300 singers, learning is accelerated. After singing a song just two or three times through, she often divides the group into parts to sing rounds. This inevitably works, even though most of us doubt that we know the song well enough to hold our part, and we fear we will let down our rounds "team" if we mess it up.

Group mind is defined as, "A collective consciousness of a group of individuals." We learn songs faster leaning on each other. This quick-study experience applies no matter who is leading, but strong songleading skills help. Lisa, Kate, and Melanie champion the confidence that the group will be able to do as they ask.

In her TED talk, "How Oral Tradition Singing Helps Us Live and Work Better Together," Barbara McAfee demonstrates group mind by leading a song and then removing herself from the equation to allow a group of strangers to decide when to stop singing.[38] Without fail, the group stops singing at exactly the same time. Focus on the song unites her audience, enabling them to act as a cohesive group.

Laurence Cole's layered songs have parts with different lyrics, melodies, and harmonies. Thinking about the complexity interferes with the process of learning the dizzying multi-part songs. To ease anxiety about the challenge, we lean on each other as we learn our parts. Even when we are not conscious we are riding the wave; group mind connects us to the other singers.

Singing in Service

It has been my experience that the bonds that develop when we sing in community are amplified when singing in service. United by the mission, bedside singers share a higher purpose. The compassionate songs we sing comfort listeners and singers alike. Blending our voices without the need to be heard above one another, a practice Sudie Pollock calls "listening louder than we sing," creates an opening to step away from the need for recognition and ego.

Kate's efforts to create pathways to service and bring song medicine to those in need led her to start a weekly singing circle with the women incarcerated in the Marin County Jail. In 2007, Karen DeTore joined Kate and a team of Threshold Choir singers at the jail, and she was deeply touched by the gratitude and generosity she witnessed there. Karen spoke of seeing one of the women banging a single cellophane-wrapped peppermint candy on the edge of her wooden chair so she could share the splintered pieces with those sitting around her in the circle. One of the incarcerated women shared that awkward silences during her weekly phone call with her teenage daughter ended when she started teaching her the songs she was learning and the calls became a time for the two of them to sing together. Karen and Kate expressed how much they missed the magic that happened singing with the women in that circle when the privatization of the county jail shut down the singing.

In 2013, Kate started a monthly sing with the men at San Quentin State Prison that Karen began leading three years later. A group of singers assembled from different Threshold Choirs in the Bay Area brought songs that included inspiring music like Coco Love Alcorn's "Good News," compassionate Threshold Choir songs, and songs written by choir members specifically for the incarcerated men. Sometimes the men would teach songs they had written. The lyrics were projected on a monitor or taught using call and response. To make the sessions inclusive, one choir member wrote Spanish translations for many of those songs.

Even with seventy-five men in the room, Karen said a reverent silence was held after each song. There were requests for favorite songs and sometimes requests to sing for friends who were struggling within the prison walls. Touched by the Holly Near song, "Singing for Our Lives," one of the men asked Karen what those words meant to her. He explained that to the men incarcerated in San Quentin, singing is as close as it gets to the connection and intimacy they crave.

"The men would come for a peaceful evening, for connection, and because they wanted to create something beautiful." Karen asks, "What else besides singing together can bring such joy in just a few minutes?"

No physical contact is permitted within the prisons. With boundaries strictly observed, the authentic connection made with the participants is purely the result of singing together. In the prison setting, the visitors, counselors, medical personnel, attorneys, and guards all have knowledge of prisoners' histories and crimes. Karen considers it a blessing to know nothing about the men and women they were singing with, "Not knowing brings a level of comfort all around."

She never feared for her safety. Karen said the incarcerated men and women were appreciative, respectful and protective. Helen Greenspan, a member of the Threshold Singers of the East Bay confided, "Singing at San Quentin, I don't know that I have ever felt so loved in my life."

COVID-19 ended the singing in San Quentin, and

by the summer of 2020, more than 2,200 of the 3,300 men incarcerated there were infected with the virus. The singing made a difference in the lives of those living within prison walls and to those who brought this gift to them. The songs and the kindness shared by those singers live on and are carried forward like ripples on still water.

CHAPTER 9

Toward the Sunrise

Following the songleaders' retreat, it was time to get back on the road and resume my mission. It lifts one's spirit to travel the inland highways of California during the winter months when gently rolling hills vibrate with new growth.

In arid California, dormant seeds wait for the first precious drops of winter rain to spring forth from the dry soil and carpet the land with verdant life. Each humble blade of grass rises to the occasion, doing its part to hold topsoil in place and guide rainwater down into the thirsty earth. By mid-April, when other parts of the country are greening, warm sunny days in the West dry the grasses, transitioning the landscape from flourishing green to the sleeping lion hills Kate Wolf sings about in "Here in California." It gives me joy to witness the full glory of the chlorophyll flush in these hills and valleys during this narrow window of time.

North of Santa Barbara, I spent two nights at Jalama Beach campground, a spot where Joe has camped with his surfer friends, and a night stealth camping on the street of a residential area. To avoid being caught sleeping in my vehicle on a public street, an early morning departure landed me at Santa Barbara's Stearns Wharf in time for a fiery sunrise. So taken by the view of elegant palm-lined streets, the calm bay ringed by chiseled mountains, and the intense crimson light rising from the horizon, I forgot the sailor's maxim, "Red sky at night, sailor's delight. Red sky in morning, sailor take warning." And warning it was.

The choir member's home where I was to stay following the Santa Barbara Threshold Singers' practice that evening is in the hills south of town where the weather forecast threatened early morning rainfall of up to two inches per hour and wind gusts up to 80 MPH. The storm forecast for February 2, 2019, combined with a two-year-old fire scar above Montecito, was a recipe for flash flooding. Even though Carol's house is on a hillside above the floodplain, the access road would be closed when the creek below swelled with rain. The storm forced me to book a hotel room near the downtown practice hall, where I hoped the protected parking lot would shelter Wanda from high winds and trees that might be downed by the storm.

Singing together with new and old friends at the practice that evening provided a reprieve from my worries about the storm brewing outside. Impressed with the bond that exists among the age diverse members of this group, it was clear their tradition of setting time aside at practices for members to share what is going on in their lives feeds that connection. I left the practice feeling held as I faced the rain, which was falling in earnest as I made my way to my hotel room.

The wind and rain did not reach the levels predicted that night, but the storm flooded downtown streets, overflowed creeks and closed Highway 101 in both directions the next day. At sunset, the highway was opened to southbound traffic and I was able to drive to Carol's, where I was made to feel like one of the family. A pianist as well as a singer, Carol and her visiting son, Jeff, an accomplished trumpet player, made sweet music together after breakfast each morning. Jeff confided that these morning concerts were bittersweet, the first since his father, Charlie, the clarinet player in their family trio, passed away last year. Carol enjoys hosting guests, and my visit followed Kate Munger's visit a week before I arrived. I was sad to leave my new friends after two days and nights of family, music, meaningful conversation, delicious meals, and ruthlessly competitive games of gin rummy.

When it was time to leave, Jeff guided me out of the driveway into the busy street. As enthusiastic as he was about my travel plans, Carol's son let me know that he felt something was missing. His parting words included advice to make space for love on this journey. By love, he was referring to romance. I did not have the time, or the words, to explain to him that this journey was all about love. Making the effort to show up was a way for me to demonstrate the love and admiration I have for those who open hearts with compassionate singing at bedsides and beyond. If the appreciation I had received from Threshold Choir members so far was any indication of what was to come, there would be no shortage of connection, bonding, and love ahead. The journey promised a more inclusive love than what Jeff was promoting.

At this time in my life, the need for the kind of attachment Jeff spoke of does not drive me. Without feeling a need to up the ante with more attention, more intimacy, and more love, my heart has opened to love that is free from expectations. It took many years to move from a place of judging my self-worth by who loved me, to loving myself enough not to need that validation. With the wisdom afforded by old age, and some help from post-menopausal hormonal changes, I may have arrived.

This pilgrimage would generate the kind of satisfying heartfelt connections that singing together in community and in service to others inspire.

A Detour

Speeding through the places where I grew up in Southern California, I felt little nostalgic pull. My only detour from congested freeways was a tour through the sprawling 1950s subdivision where my grandmother and two great aunts once lived within blocks of each other. In a family dedicated to closely held secrets, I prized the time spent with my great aunties who knew no such constraints. They spoke freely to me about all matters, including the regular visits they received from their long deceased mother. Great Aunt Anna Mae tutored me in couturier seamstress skills the summer following my grandmother's passing.

A platinum blonde in white marabou mules with the heft and determination of a Sumo wrestler, Anna Mae was awe-inspiring. She was an entrepreneur with a yard filled with aviaries and nesting boxes that vibrated with the chatter of cockatiels, canaries, and finches. Indoors, immense aquariums housed little fan-tailed guppies dutifully reproducing multitudes of tiny offspring which Anna Mae sold to pet stores. The state-of-the-art sewing room where she expertly pieced together everything from tailored suits to beaded gowns for Nancy Dinsmore, the West Coast Editor of *Harper's Bazaar* magazine, was not my only classroom that summer.

Arriving at the house early each morning to help with the day's cleaning and baking chores, great Aunt Tilly's kindness lit every room she entered. In flowery dresses gathered at her tiny waist, she was a slender bird darting in and out of Anna Mae's impressive shadow, smoothing the feathers ruffled by her less benevolent sister. She was not there to intervene the day a misguided driver yelled profanities at Anna Mae when we were stuck in LA traffic with babies to deliver to the fish store. In response, my auntie reached for the giant crescent wrench stashed under her seat, stepped out of her car, and wielded the mighty plumbing implement over her head daring the driver to repeat his slur. He did not.

In the afternoons, Anna Mae's white Formica kitchen table was the gathering place for wrinkled, world-wise women with loose tongues, rolled-down stockings, and bony fingers stacked with diamond rings that signified a lifetime of husbands, come and gone. Survivors of wars, the Great Depression, bus driving, chorus line dancing, love, loss, and youth, these were women who knew some things, and this thirteen-year-old was all ears. Grace, one of my aunts' devoted posse, roared in on her motorcycle to join the gang each afternoon. With short cropped hair and flannel shirts with rolled-up sleeves, she didn't exactly blend. These plucky elders weren't bound by the gender roles that defined my mother. In Anna Mae's kitchen, all but the fainthearted were welcome.

Driving the neighborhood some fifty years later, no hint of that history was visible. I envy people with roots in their childhood homes, but I feel no connection to the densely populated valleys of Southern California where I grew up longing for the sea.

Riverside, California, my next stop, took me further away from my Pacific Coast comfort zone. The region's orange groves, palm-lined streets, and boulder-covered hills gave me the feeling I had traveled back in time to the California of my early childhood. The reception I received from the RiverSong Threshold Choir made me feel like a hero. A visit from Melanie DeMore launched this choir. Jerri, the founder of the chapter, first reached out to her when her sister was dying. Melanie helped soothe the passing by singing over the phone in her rich bass voice. Jerri, a talented vocalist and choir director, was inspired by the experience.

Barbara, the co-leader of RiverSong, lived in Pacific Grove before returning to Riverside to care for her mother. She sent me off the next morning with a hearty breakfast, warm wishes, and cash for my gas fund. Heading east, I faced the unknown fueled up and feeling supported.

Mindfully

With five days to reach my next choir stop in San Antonio, Texas, Picacho Peak State Park in Arizona was the only scheduled stop on my itinerary. I prefer driving slowly, with plenty of time to take in the scenery and stops to stretch and explore towns, historic sites, and parks every couple of hours. Three to four hours behind the wheel in one day is ideal for me; the ten-hour stretches on this leg of the journey were a strain. Singing along to MaMuse, Carole King, Joan Baez, Bobby McFerrin, Laurence Cole, and Wholehearted Chorus CDs kept me in good spirits despite the long hours behind the wheel.

As I continued east on Highway 10, the vast wind and solar farms of the California desert disappeared, as did all signs of civilization other than frenetic Love's and

Pilot truck stops. As scenery and vegetation grew sparse, gusty winds increased. At times, the driving demanded ferocious concentration as dangerous traffic conditions, wind, stretches of rough road, and the vacuum that pulled me towards the next lane when a truck passed, kept my body on full alert. Even though I frequently reminded myself to drop tension-raised shoulders and relax my jaw, clenched teeth on this stretch of lonely highway resulted in a broken tooth.

To stay alert, I developed an afternoon nap routine that would recharge my energy throughout the journey. It's not that napping is new to me; ten-minute power naps got me through years of working long hours, and sometimes three jobs, as a single mother. Sleep comes easily for me in the middle of the day, especially following a satisfying lunch and sleepless night. My body responds well to this routine. After pulling over to prepare and eat my lunch, I enjoyed surrendering to the delicious drowsiness that came over me. Moving to my "bedroom," I stretched out and fell into a deep sleep. Ten minutes is all it takes for me to wake up feeling refreshed and ready to drive on. Napping wasn't reserved strictly for lunchtime, either. Anytime driving in the warm sun made me sleepy, I would find a place to pull off the road and take a snooze, because I could.

The practice of being present gave meaning to each mile. Many decades ago, a teacher pointed out how fulfilling life can be when we fully engage with each precious moment. She described how we often drift un-focused, using the example of arriving at a destination by car, surprised to be there and not remembering passing familiar landmarks along the way. On this stretch of the journey, tuning in to the endless blue skies, wide open expanses, and far-reaching vistas of the desert gave me a new appreciation for the spaciousness of this arid land.

My friend, Elayne, gave me a copy of Mary Oliver's poem, *Mindful*,[39] to carry with me on the journey. I found the poem a valuable reminder to look, to listen, and to appreciate every aspect of this grand adventure. I learned the verses by heart and practiced aloud until the poem was part of me, much like the songs that live within us.

The weirdly animated limbs of the saguaro cactus heralded my arrival in Arizona. Because I was moving too fast to spot living wildlife, dead critters at the side of the road offered clues to the inhabitants of this strange territory. I occupied myself inventorying roadkill. Sadly, on one stretch of highway, I counted four dead coyotes, one opossum, three rabbits, a peccary (a three-foot-long pig-like cactus-eater that I had to identify online), and one armadillo that landed on its back with stiff little legs and tiny feet standing straight up in the air. "All God's Critters Got a Place in the Choir" was the theme song for this stretch of the journey.

Spring-like conditions in the winter draw campers in Airstreams and kitschy retro trailers to Arizona's Picacho Peak State Park (yes, this is redundant, *picacho* is Spanish for *peak*). My reservation was timed to coincide with a singing cowboy performance at the park.

An open-air amphitheater with a spectacular cactus-peppered mountain backdrop was the perfect setting for a sunset songfest. The former doo-wop singer confessed he was no cowboy, even though he looked the part. No matter, the setting and the singing were grand. In a deep resonant voice, he sang "Cool Water," "Ghost Riders in the Sky,""Tumbling Tumble Weeds," and other traditional Western favorites, songs that are old friends. The audience was transported to the romantic Old West that this music conjures for generations of Americans. We knew all the words and happily sang along. The starry night that followed the show was too dazzling to waste on sleep.

Still singing cowboy songs, I headed out the next day, making a short stop in the historic district of Tucson. I took in the art museum and enjoyed being introduced to the fabulous up-town, yet distinctly Western style of this city. I encountered the best chili relleno I have ever tasted at a trendy outdoor café near the art museum. Crisp on the outside, the egg-battered chili was served on a pool of red and green sauces that were so good, I devoured a full basket of chips scooping up every drop.

It was disappointing not to have time to check in with the Phoenix and Tucson Threshold Choirs, but I had a schedule to keep. An appointment with the San Antonio chapter kept me moving. As my journey progressed, I became less willing to plan ahead, opting for more room for spontaneity. It would take many months to comprehend the freedom available to me.

After a long day of driving, it was dark when I found a spectacular rest stop on a mesa overlooking Las Cruces, New Mexico. The town is named for the graves of settlers who lost their lives in the terrible ethnic cleansing we know as the Indian Wars. The stylish overlook was built in a circle with round picnic shelters constructed of desert stone and parking that looked down on the lights of the city far below. I couldn't believe my good luck to land free parking where the sparkling view rivalled the best accommodations money can buy.

Moving through time as well as through space, I entered the third time zone I would occupy in a six-day period when I crossed the Texas state line. In San Antonio, I settled into my driveway digs in the shade of the enormous oaks outside Cay's lovely studio home. My timing proved to be excellent. I was invited to attend practices for both San Antonio Threshold Choir chapters, and to participate in segments of the training video the choir director, Deborah, was producing for the TCI organization. This dedicated director started a second San Antonio Threshold Choir at a large retirement community to enable the elderly choir members living there to attend practices without the expense of a taxi ride across town. Choir members embedded within this retirement community are available to provide bedside singing for the inhabitants whenever there is a need. The time I spent with Cay was enlightening, and I'm grateful for the shared meals and the tour of San Antonio's exciting Riverwalk at night.

Alligators and Accordions

Veering south as I traveled to my next choir stop in New Orleans, I checked into a campground that boasts miles of bayous with more than 300 adult alligators. On my first day at Brazos Bend State Park, I spotted an owl, white and purple ibis, two turtles, a garter snake, and two alligators. During an evening walk around one of the lakes, I encountered a six-foot gator sunning itself next to the walking trail. The couple ahead continued on the path, passing within two feet of the resting creature, I reversed direction, creeped-out by the beast's size and toothy grin.

This campground had it all. I added a third night to reorganize my belongings and use the laundromat. Temperatures in the 80s required unpacking my flip flops and the summer clothes that were tightly crammed into the van's storage compartments. I brought along a travel steamer for occasions like this. Taking advantage of the electricity at my campsite, I hung wrinkled cotton and linen clothing from tree branches and steamed my wardrobe for the next several months. Yes, it felt ridiculous to be carrying on like this in camp, but living on the road has its quirks, and I have my standards.

Seventy-six-year-old Nancy, a very friendly full-time Roadtreker who was a camp neighbor, told me she has been on the road for more than two years. When asked where she would go next, she told me she doesn't plan ahead, she follows the road. Impromptu entertainment on the last night was a surprise. Musicians in the next campsite played enchanting tango music on accordions.

Mosquito Wars

Lured by the prospect of primitive camping on the beach, I took a ferry to the Bolivar Peninsula on the Gulf Coast of Texas. Alone on miles of fog shrouded beach at Sea Rim State Park, I discovered this was not as liberating as I had imagined. The vision of being carried off by high tide prompted me to periodically turn on my headlamps to check the water level throughout the night.

Settling in to do some writing at sunset, I was shocked to see the windows were black with swarms of hungry mosquitoes trying to get inside. I calmed myself with the thought that I was safe in the watertight van, but I was mistaken. After hours of lost sleep swatting at the pests buzzing in my ears, I got out of bed and dug through my belongings to find the three-year-old herbal mosquito repellent I had purchased in Bali, and the spot remover I had packed. Spraying myself and my bedding with the cinnamony potion and cleaning blood stains from the upholstered walls around my bed where I had smashed the intruders did not bring sleep, as I hoped it would.

Sleepless Night on the Gulf Coast.

Vending Machine Pickles

Upon reaching Louisiana, I explored Lake Pontchartrain, camped on Tchefuncte River, and visited St. Francisville before making my way to New Orleans. I have spent time in Louisiana before, both as a tourist and working for

FEMA. The colorful blend of humanity, music, food, language, and culture is intriguing, and the wildlife rich waterways, historic buildings, and lichen-draped oaks cast an alluring dream-like spell.

It was an honor to join the NOLA Threshold Choir in New Orleans for a practice and bedside singing. The music director is meticulous about the sound of the choir, and they bring their gift to three hospice facilities each week, offer bedside singing at other locations monthly, and show up for requests from the community.

This chapter, much like the chapter in San Antonio, serves patients as visitors, not hospice volunteers. That arrangement made it possible for me to join them at bedsides without official hospice volunteer status. Opportunities to sing at bedsides were rare, and I sorely missed regular participation in the service aspect of Threshold Choir while traveling. On the other hand, meeting with an entire chapter when they are practicing allowed for dialogue, song sharing, and a "tribal" experience that is not the focus at bedsides. I am grateful for both.

In New Orleans, I enjoyed shrimp "po boy" sandwiches and many hours of story swapping with Hermene before moving downtown to Jeanne and Leigh's home, where I learned the customary crawfish eating technique. My arrival happened to coincide with Mardi Gras and I joined revelers at spirited parades celebrating the unique music and frivolities. A presentation given by local and Haitian Voodoo priests and priestesses at the Museum of Art included the traditional drumming and dancing that has a strong presence here in New Orleans. I left NOLA grateful for my gracious new friends and fresh insights into the citys' intoxicating culture. Invited to visit Jeanne and Leigh's "camp" (beach house, in California lingo), I headed south to the Gulf Coast and sleepy Grand Isle. The island took a direct hit from Hurricane Ida in 2021, I was relieved to learn that my friends' house, which stands on stilts sixteen feet high, survived the storm.

A Waffle House every few blocks, graceful mansions with large expanses of unfenced lawns, vending machine pickles, and unabashed good manners were indicators I was in the deep South as I followed the coast through Mississippi and Alabama en route to Florida. Beautiful stretches of sugar sand beaches greeted me along the gulf coast. After a traditional dinner of southern fried chicken and canned green beans, I spent a night next to the water in a casino parking lot on Biloxi Bay where I enjoyed a spectacular view of the arch of lights on the bridge that straddles the bay.

A walk in historic downtown Mobile the next day revealed statues that commemorate a Mardi Gras history that predates New Oleans' famous festival. A week after my visit, a deadly tornado would touch down there.

Across the Florida state line, a stop at the Welcome Center was an assault on the senses. Beautiful people engaged in exciting water activities flashed across multiple screens overhead while Jimmy Buffett's "Margaritaville" blared from large speakers. This well-oiled marketing machine included attractive, bronzed employees handing out free orange and grapefruit juice, and rows of shelves filled with glossy pamphlets and visitor magazines with countless options to pay to play. I quickly moved on.

CHAPTER 10

Vulnerability

As I continued east along Florida's panhandle, the sight of miles of forests flattened, domino fashion, was a clue that this state is a magnet for violent weather. I arrived in Tallahassee at dusk and followed back roads to the Miccosukee Land Cooperative to settle in among the pines and amaryllis blooms where Georjean, a member of the Tallahassee Threshold Choir, kindly offered parking.

Conversation over morning coffee with Georjean and her husband, Cliff, on their deck overlooking the woods was inspiring. We shared songs and stories, and when asked how long it had taken to build their three-story home, Cliff answered that he started in 1974, and is still at it. When he told me Georjean had nixed the tower he wanted to add to the top floor, I shared my pictures of Robinson Jeffers' Hawk Tower at Tor House in Carmel, where I was once a docent, and read Jeffers' poem, "Hurt Hawks."[40] Cliff shared some of his poetry.

Georjean's artwork adorns the walls of the home, and when I asked about a painting of a hawk, she told me her brother painted it. The painting was hanging over the window where a hawk perched for three days when he died, and she said she still has no idea what the bird found to perch on outside the window.

Joining the Tallahassee Area Threshold Singers for their last practice of the month, I was in time for their regular social gathering that includes a "covered dish," Southern speak for "potluck." After talking and eating for an hour, the director sounded a chime, followed by a meditation that set the tone for an hour of singing. Susan directed the singing with clear, supportive, and inclusive leadership, and I could feel the bond that exists among the members. The five-year-old chapter has deep roots in Velma Frye's singing circle, and because of that, some members have been singing together for twenty years. With talented songwriters in the group, they shared some of their original bedside songs and gave me copies of their CD to give to choirs I would visit.

Susan invited me to spend a night at her home and join her the next day singing with Velma Frye.[41] I was surprised to find I knew most of the songs Velma led. The gathering with the gifted musician was followed by an afternoon of deep conversation with a member of the Tallahassee chapter discussing the vulnerability we feel aging alone as single women .

After a few days, I began feeling a chest cold coming on, and the need to isolate. Georjean invited me to stay as long as I needed to, and to help myself to the vitamin rich citrus fruit growing on the property. Behind a small wooden gate, garden paths fashioned with seashells and playful stone designs showed the way to trees heavy with ripe oranges and grapefruit. The fruit bore the taste of paradise; sunny, juicy, and revitalizing. Fireflies shimmering in the garden at night added to the magic.

Tornado Warning

This peaceful setting tested my mettle on March 3, 2019. After an evening walk on the boardwalk that meanders through the co-op's "psychedelic swamp," a squirrelly wind was rustling the treetops when I returned to the van. A hard rain began to fall as I settled in for my evening meal. The rain was followed by thunder in the distance that quickly grew closer and louder. Lightning strikes became so frequent that the darkness of night vanished behind a curtain of flashing lights.

Just when I started wondering what would happen if lightning found the tall van or hit a tree nearby, an emergency alert sounded on my phone, followed by a repeating warning: "Take immediate cover. Tornado approaching your vicinity." The image of my little home being sucked into a spinning vortex, like Dorothy's house in *The Wizard of Oz*, motivated me to seek shelter at Georjean's. I was shaking with adrenalin as I gathered essentials to bring with me.

Until this moment, I was confident I was prepared for emergencies with my training working for FEMA and as a member of a Community Emergency Response Team in Pacific Grove. The tornado warning made me realize that in the van, I had no emergency bag like the suitcase I kept packed with supplies and important papers in the front closet of my former apartment. The emergency supplies I carried were tucked away where I could find space. I hadn't considered the need to evacuate the vehicle.

In a panic, I grabbed my phone, flashlight, toothbrush, and PJs, donned rain gear, and struck out into the raging storm. I was more than a little anxious about completing the ten-minute walk to the house before the tornado struck. Like a frightened little mouse, I arrived at Georjean and Cliff's front door panting, shivering, and dripping wet, begging to shelter in the basement. My hosts were in no hurry, having been through this drill many times before. They were entertaining a dinner guest who had come to Florida to support anti-fracking groups in the area and educate legislators on the dangers of water contamination from fracking, and I had arrived in time for dessert.

After the chocolate cake, Georjean suggested we sit on the porch to listen for a sound like a freight train approaching, the signal that the tornado was near, and it was time to head downstairs. To my great relief, the household finally retreated to the basement when it became too difficult to distinguish the roar of thunder from the sound of a train approaching. Downstairs, I felt more secure, but ill-prepared. I couldn't stop picturing Wanda being carried away with my wallet, ID, the insurance paperwork, my laptop, and all the things I should have grabbed. The warning was extended several hours, but we had electricity, and followed the weather on TV.

When we received the "all clear," we learned the storm had spawned multiple tornadoes, including one that touched down twenty miles from Tallahassee. The tornadoes that hit neighboring Georgia and Alabama that night were deadly, killing twenty people and doing major damage.

The next day, a bit shaken and still feeling ill, I got the van stuck in deep mud, a result of the heavy rain. New to driving a large, heavy vehicle, my determined efforts to escape only made things worse. After forty minutes of fishtailing and wheel-spinning in the muck, Georjean's son came to the rescue with a wheelbarrow filled with gravel. I left Tallahassee to head south along

Florida's Gulf Coast with plans to visit two other choirs, family members, and the Everglades. Best made plans...

Manatees

Located on the West Coast, Manatee Springs State Park is the site of one of Florida's many crystalline thermal pools where 72° water provides a refuge for manatees. My campsite was a short walk from a clear pool where the gentle creatures rested, and a tropical wonderland where bromeliads flourish in infinite variety and cypress and slash pines are draped with tattered curtains of lichen. Despite the Vitamin C regimen, I was very ill by this time. I was wheezing, weak, and plagued with a grossly productive cough that made sleep impossible.

The prospect of being sick and alone on the road had haunted me from the moment I began planning the trip. Now that I was actually dealing with illness, I found I could manage by shifting to slow motion. Comfortable in my well-equipped home, all I needed in the way of food, water, music, and books was conveniently close. I extended my stay at Manatee Springs, and managed to venture outside for short afternoon strolls.

When it was time to move on to stay on schedule, I made a stop at an urgent care clinic. I had hoped the doctor would fix what ailed me and reassure me I wasn't contagious. The doctor did neither, of course. She prescribed an antibiotic and sent me off with a face mask. I got as far as Crystal River, another popular manatee site, and checked into a hotel, took a hot bath, ordered room service, and canceled upcoming choir visits to focus on my health. The illness was not the disaster I had imagined; in fact, it bolstered my confidence to know sickness might slow me down, but it wouldn't stop me. The need to cancel choir dates was a set-back.

I have family on Florida's east coast, and pointing Wanda eastward, I headed towards the Atlantic with Siri directing me to every toll road. I depended on GPS navigation, and for the most part, it was a reliable pilot for the 13,000 miles I had covered since October, but not on this stretch of highway. Spending $18.00 on tolls in one day, I burned through the two rolls of quarters intended for campground showers and laundromats. To make matters worse, because I had declined the offer to buy a toll pass at the garish Florida Welcome Center, I was forced to pull over at cash payment booths every twenty minutes or so. After that frustrating drive, I figured out how to program the navigation app to avoid toll roads.

My next campsite was a primitive county recreational site. It is not easy to find available campsites in Florida during high season, and this one on the St. John's River was free. I followed miles of unpaved roads through dense pine and palmetto forests to the river where a field, an outhouse, and a boat ramp were the only accommodations. An airboat was parked on the riverbank next to three forty-foot-long RVs, a couple of tents, and empty trucks and boat trailers. I claimed a patch of grass near the boat ramp as my campsite, the only place available next to the water. Opening the side doors to a fresh breeze coming from the wandering slough, I settled in for an evening meal in the soft light of a rosy sunset. Exhausted, and still dealing with bronchitis, I hunkered down for a long sleep, blissfully unaware of what the evening would bring.

Just before dark, a truck towing an airboat pulled in next to my chosen campsite, dropping the boat on the grass fifty feet from the water's edge. When the powerful engine fired up, a forceful blast of air shook the van, showering Wanda with bits of grass. Two more trucks and boats arrived, engines were tested and strips of lights bright enough to light up a small city were turned on. I saw large ice chests loaded onto boats, but no fishing poles or nets.

I found out later that this spot is a launch for nighttime alligator poachers. By the time the boats thundered back into camp just after midnight, I had relocated as far from the riverbank as I could get. Try as I would, it was too dark to see their catch.

Reaching the Atlantic

It was a beautiful sunny day when I reached Cocoa Beach on the Space Coast and stepped into a full-on summer beach scene. I reached the Atlantic nearly six months after starting my trip on the Pacific Coast and I joined happy families and dogs playing in the warm ocean. My youngest sister has lived on Merritt Island since my parents relocated there when she was in high school.

My nature loving family left Southern California for a riverfront property near Cocoa Beach, drawn by the diversity of wildlife Florida offers. The thrill of spotting alligators, flamingos, roseate spoonbills, herons, dolphins, and manatees is not lost on me. Ever since my first visit to this wet and wild land, I find myself looking for gators in waterways wherever I go. After spending a few days catching up with Sally and her husband, Erik, I drove an hour south to my middle sister's home in Sebastian.

By the time I reached Sharon's house, a drop in engine oil pressure signaled a problem. Just as my health improved, Wanda got sick. This would be a major repair that required a ten-day wait for an opening in the shop that would do the work. The delay extended my stay with Sharon and her partner, Tommy, and forced me to cancel my camping reservation at Everglades National Park.

Determined not to miss the next practice of the Sarasota Threshold Choir, I rented a car for the three-hour drive back across the state, and after a night in a Sarasota hotel, I was able to join members of the Threshold Choir for a potluck and singing. Linda, the choir director, offered her home for the next night's stay. Taking time to share songs, life stories, and personal challenges was a precious experience that made the trip to Sarasota more than worthwhile. I'm still disappointed the timing didn't work out for rescheduling with The Villages Threshold Choir.

Once the van repair was completed, I headed north to Jacksonville, where the Hanna Beach Campground provided the perfect setting for campfire dinners with my grown nephews, Joey and Johnny. When my plan to make my way north from Jacksonville to sing with the Threshold Singers of Beaufort, North Carolina, didn't work out, I headed back to Tallahassee for another visit with friends made there.

During the visit, Georjean set me up in her studio so I could join her creating a Milagrito, a form of Mexican folk art giving thanks for miracles that have occurred. Georjean, whose dream paintings speak directly to spirit, recreated a dream of her daughter who was tragically killed in a car accident when she was seventeen years old. Her Milagrito depicts an angelic young woman with flowing hair walking on a beach with a distinctive arrowhead necklace hanging from her neck. Georjean explained that after that dream, she was walking on the beach when the arrowhead her daughter wore in that dream washed up at her feet. I painted the miracle of my son rising from the bottom of Tehauntepec River and returning to life. Miracles do happen.

Navigating the Complicated South

The opportunity to sing with choirs in Georgia and South Carolina drew me on. Seeing the picturesque South for the first time during the spectacular bloom of spring, how could I help but fall in love with the beauty of this part of the country? I followed back roads through pine forests, orchards, and alongside the black waters of the Suwanee River to what I expected to be the home of a member of the Heart of Georgia Threshold Choir. Where agricultural lands gave way to an abandoned cotton field, I came to a dusty lot where dozens of FEMA-style trailer homes stood, dented and damaged by storms. The trailers offer shelter from the elements that people living on the streets in tarps and tents don't have, but the hopelessness of an endless cycle of generational poverty could be felt in the air. Kids walking home from school glared at this outsider who knew nothing of their struggles.

Driving deeper into the neighborhood, I passed a mix of well-cared-for mobile homes on landscaped lots and neglected trailers. Continuing to follow Siri's directions, I turned onto a long dirt driveway where overgrown shrubs made for a tight fit for the Roadtrek. At the end of the drive, I found myself in a clearing with abandoned cars and a double-wide in disrepair. I was sitting in my vehicle gathering my thoughts when I began to see this as an opportunity to get to know a choir member whose life and perspective would be so different from my own. Ready to charge ahead with that anticipation, I opened the van door to a sea of trash and liquor bottles littering the path to the badly damaged front door.

It became clear to me that if this home was occupied, and that was a big "if," the residents were likely engaged in a very real struggle to survive. It occurred to me that the privilege to volunteer for worthy causes like Threshold Choir is not available to all. Forced to make a judgment call, I reckoned that no Threshold Choir member lived in this trailer (this, from a choir member who was living in driveways and rest stops in a van). My gut told me I was in the wrong place, I would not be welcome here, and if someone drove up the narrow driveway behind me, I would be trapped. I made a safe exit, but I'm still uncomfortable about making a judgment about who would or wouldn't be a Threshold Choir singer.

As it turned out, Siri had directed me to the right address in the wrong town. An hour, and a few phone calls later, I located the charming Macon neighborhood that was my destination. Hetty was waiting for me, and I was pleased to be reminded of the delightful conversation we shared over morning coffee at a Threshold Choir gathering in California years before. Macon impressed me with its tree-lined residential neighborhoods, lavish gardens, and the grand Greek Revival architecture that graces downtown. I spent two nights in Hetty's driveway. A beautiful evening singing with the Heart of Georgia Threshold Choir led to a pub meal seasoned with plenty of laughter following the practice.

Leaving Hetty and gorgeous Macon, I made a stop in Savannah before heading to South Carolina. Spring was in full bloom as I passed fields ablaze in red wildflowers, pecan orchards with tiny green buds, and fragrant wisteria draping the forests in violet. Some of those flowering vines climbed thirty feet up into the pines. In Savannah's historic district, I walked cobbled streets and oak shaded public squares admiring the charming architecture and reading plaques that told of the city's distinguished past. I did not join the three blocks long line of folks waiting to dine at The Olde Pink House. Although history reins in Savanah, the city is not impervious to change. The forty-eight foot tall Confederate Monument erected in 1875 was rededicated to all who died in the Civil War in 2018.

In early April, the giant RV "Resorts" and surf shops of Myrtle Beach, South Carolina, had not yet opened for the summer season. I camped in a tangle of forest at the State Park where signs warned it was coral snake habitat. The signs also advised that the snake's tiny mouth makes their deadly venom a threat only to campers whose toes are exposed in sandals or flip flops. Sneakers it was.

The Long Bay Threshold Singers' director took me under her wing, hiking park trails with me and showing me the innovative new housing and retail developments in town. We ate at an Asian fusion restaurant that felt more like dining in San Francisco than South Carolina. Well done, Myrtle Beach. Joining the choir practice, I appreciated Cynthia's skilled and kindhearted direction. After stretches and warm-up exercises, members chose a song to lead. If they were not comfortable leading, they were encouraged to ask another member to lead the song.

A hard rain flooding the highway caused the van to hydroplane as I left Myrtle Beach to head for Asheville, North Carolina. The weather radar map indicated clear weather to the west, so I proceeded to Columbia, South Carolina, the halfway point, and the location of a Cracker Barrel restaurant where I could park overnight.

If you haven't traveled in the South, you might not know this chain of restaurants. Much like Waffle Houses, Cracker Barrels are an institution in these parts. Serving down-home food at reasonable prices, the restaurants are popular with locals and tourists. The busy décor includes rocking chairs on the front porch, an excessive amount of "old-time" signage, Dolly Parton music, and a retail store selling all manner of "cute."

At the time I traveled, most of the 665 restaurants in the chain provided RV parking spots where guests could stay the night without charge. This would my first of sixteen overnights at Cracker Barrels in ten states, and it felt like I was staying at a resort. The friendly staff was welcoming, it was a good distance from the highway, and the manicured lawns created a buffer between the parking lot and the nearest neighbors, a Hyatt hotel on one side, and a Doubletree on the other. I passed the night quietly, grateful for the free overnight, and for Cracker Barrel's tasty berry cobbler.

Feral Leanings

In trendy Asheville, North Carolina, a fresh feeling in
the air signaled I had reached the Blue Ridge Mountains.
Bustling with activity, art, and tattooed wild-haired
youth, Ashville is the Portland of the South. Repurposed
warehouses along the river are home to a vibrant art and
craft beer scene. Venturing into the studio of a brilliant
young artist whose intricate paintings transported me
to other worlds, I learned she had relocated from San
Francisco four years earlier with her ex-husband who
grew up in the area. Instead of "ex-husband," Cat referred
to him as her "wasband," a term worthy of passing on.

Parked in the driveway of a choir member who is
a young single mother, I learned about her struggle to
find affordable housing for her family in this desirable
city where booming tourism and demand for vacation
homes has skyrocketed rents. A familiar story. Singing
and sharing songs with the Asheville Threshold Choir at
the cooperative community where some of the members
live was comforting, especially the stretches and circle
shoulder rub that kicked off the practice. The leaders
were quick to adopt Eleanor Decker's lifted hand song
closing. I was invited to join members for a delicious
Indian dinner afterward.

From Asheville, I headed toward the Great Smoky
Mountains National Park with a stop in Waynesville to
have lunch with Mary, a Threshold Choir singer in that
little town. Mary is an accomplished Reiki Master, Death

Doula, and New Age minister, as well as a Threshold Choir director. She told me she regularly drives to Asheville to provide Reiki treatments and singing for the occupants of homeless shelters there because the citizens of her little mountain town have no interest in her services.

Before settling into my campsite in the National Park, I explored the town of Cherokee at the park entrance. In this touristy seat of the Cherokee Nation, you can purchase a dreamcatcher with flamingo pink feathers, a velvet Elvis Presley painting, a Dukes of Hazzard poster, or a henna tattoo. There is also a downtown casino. The timing did not work out to see the play, "Unto These Hills," that portrays the history of the Cherokee in this land, how Manifest Destiny affected indigenous people, and the tragedy of the Trail of Tears. At the park's Visitor Center, photos of families who lost their generational homes to the National Park show that even public ownership of land comes at a cost to those who made homes there.

The Smokemont Campground in the Great Smoky Mountains National Park offered sweet smelling wildflowers, a spectacular night sky, the music of rushing streams, and the surprise of elk wandering through the campsite, it did not offer showers. A warm morning allowed me to use the van's outside shower nozzle to wash my hair outdoors in the sunshine.

By this point in the journey, I was leaning towards feral. Going days without seeing another human, combined with a problematic shower set-up inside the van and minimal access to laundry facilities, led to a change in my hygiene.

With the exception of underwear, which I had room to pack in great abundance, I wore the same clothes day in and day out. My former routine of starting each day with a shower gave way to a shower when kind choir members offered the opportunity, or when I was lucky enough to find a campground with facilities. Sponge baths and bathroom wipes got me through the in-between times. When heat and humidity made bathing critical, I stuck close to lakes and rivers where I could cool off and bathe at the same time. I had planned my trip around the perimeter of the country in an effort not to stray too far from the water.

To reduce the need for professional grooming, I grew my hair long for the trip, usually wearing it in braids or a ponytail, and often neglecting to comb it unless I would be seen in public. I frequently discovered I was wearing my shirt inside-out. My personal metamorphosis was a precursor to the widespread change in personal habits to come with COVID-19 shelter-in-place orders.

The Barber of Sylva

After taking in the remarkable scenery of the National Park lands, I headed to the historic courthouse-turned-library in the picturesque mountain hamlet of Sylva that Mary encouraged visiting. Once I was finished posting a blog entry, making travel arrangements, and down-loading Audio Books, I toured the building and grounds of the majestic hilltop structure. Making my way to the impressive stairs at the entry, I was confronted by Sylva Sam, a thirty-foot-tall statue commemorating Confederate soldiers that lords over the town.

The profound beauty of the South is intoxicating, and the hospitality, quaint little towns, and arts and crafts are charming, but as sweet as it is, sorrow and heartbreak weigh on the soul of this place. I am one of many who feel sadness and despair seeing the veneration of those who fought to maintain the brutal institution of slavery. The Civil War battlefields, monuments, and cemeteries in this region often brought me to tears. In discussions with choir members who live where Confederate statues have come down, they expressed a wish to keep the statues of their ancestors on display, suggesting that statues of Civil Rights heroes and other champions of racial and social justice be erected for a more balanced account of history.

Fortified by a bowl of soup at Sylva's bohemian City Lights Bookstore, I explored the tiny downtown. At the end of Main Street, an old fashioned barbershop with a sign, "Men's $10.00 Haircuts," caught my eye.

Badly in need of a haircut, and having just washed my hair at my campsite, it occurred to me this was the ideal time for a quick trim, something accomplished in ten minutes at Supercuts in Monterey.

Despite the word "Men's" that was clearly indicated on the sign, I took a deep breath, squared my shoulders, and entered the flag-draped shop where customers waited on worn Naugahyde bench seating that appeared to have been retrieved from old pickup trucks. Friendly Vance, one of two barbers, sported Birkenstocks, a head wrap, and a man bun. His appearance was in sharp contrast to the other barber at the shop; a dapper, white-haired Southern gentleman who wore a classic linen suit and a waxed handlebar mustache.

The older barber, clearly nervous about my presence in this sanctuary of masculinity, hesitantly told me he doesn't know how to cut women's hair. Vance was up for the challenge, so I sat down and waited my turn. When the cut ahead of me was completed, the kind barber refused payment, saying how glad he was to see the customer. Some polite back-and-forth followed, with insistence that Vance accept the $12.00 payment offered. Until this point, I wasn't sure haircuts really were $10.00, thinking the sign might have been retained purely for its historical value.

When it was my turn in the chair, Vance carefully divided my hair into sections and went to work. This was not going to be a Supercuts trim. He began asking questions, curious about what had brought this stranger to his town and this shop. He was very interested in my Threshold Choir tour and announced he is looking forward to death.

The usual response when I talk about Threshold Choir singing is either a shrug with a statement that the listener could never do something like that, or an emotional gush of gratitude for the service. When I asked Vance to explain his comment, he shared his theory that death would offer a release from time. With five kids and a family farm to tend, I imagine his time is in great demand. After hearing his story, I shared that in *Anam Cara*, John O'Donohue writes about death and time, saying with death we transcend the pressures of linear time for the freedom of eternal time.[42] After a good hour of cutting and conversing, Vance refused payment, telling me the last customer had paid ahead. He thanked me for coming into his life, wrote down John O'Donohue's name, and gave me a hug.

The barber of Sylva is a bridge builder. I was touched by his kindness, and his ease breaking down barriers between strangers from different worlds.

Seeking Safe Harbor

When clouds resting on the mountaintops obscured the road, I had to leave the Blue Ridge Parkway and head down the mountain. Driving lonely Highway 81, a tornado warning had me scanning the shoulder for a place to park the van and lie face down in a ditch or swale with my arms covering my head, as I had read should be done if a tornado approaches when you are on the road. I didn't like this plan. With no tornadoes or ditches in sight, I opted to take shelter at a Subway shop at the next off-ramp. It was business as usual inside, so I ordered food I was too nervous to eat, and monopolized a large table with the overstuffed emergency bag I had assembled after my scare in Tallahassee. With everything but the kitchen sink loaded into the bag, I could shift my focus from keeping my things safe to keeping my body safe.

At the Subway shop, I watched fearless customers come and go as if there was no disaster looming (which, fortunately, turned out to be the case). Deadly tornadoes hit Texas that day and the same weather system was expected to reach my destination, Roanoke, Virginia, the following afternoon. A stormy spring and early summer produced swarms of tornadoes along my route from Florida to Minnesota, making 2019 the fourth most active tornado season to date.

A fortune cookie with the message, "You're not afraid of storms, for you're learning to sail your ship" fell into my hands at a Chinese restaurant somewhere along this route, and I took it as a sign. The affirmation, a quote from Louisa May Alcott (since when do fortune cookies contain quotes from western literature?), continued to bring me comfort when tornado warnings sent me scurrying to avoid a predicted path of destruction. My strategy was not altogether effective, as three of those capricious twisters touched down within thirty miles of where I had driven to avoid them. Still, I'm here to tell the story.

Continuing on, I explored Virginia's farm country, rolling hills, classic farmhouses, and barns while trying to stay out of the haphazard path of tornadoes. This kind of vulnerability made me feel very alone. I was swimming in open water; no one could tell me where to find safe harbor with storms threatening the entire South and mid-Atlantic region. Stopping for an overnight in Roanoke, I rushed out of the Cracker Barrel parking lot at 5:00 a.m., following radar maps to stay ahead of the weather.

Fleeing to Richmond, Virginia, I checked into a hotel room while the city waited for the storm. Hotels provided shelter and the ability to follow weather reports on TV. That night, it wasn't looking good. Preparing the van as best I could, I covered the windows and brought my go bag and food indoors. Deployed with FEMA, I have seen the pressure of tornadoes cause car windows to implode and shower the interior with shattered glass. After a tremendous clap of thunder and heavy rain woke me, several storm cells passed over in the wee morning hours bringing heavy rain, thunder, and lightning. Richmond escaped damage from the fast-moving storms that day, but within a forty-eight hour period, high winds and sixteen tornadoes caused deaths and major damage from Texas to Pennsylvania.

Waking up to sunshine after the rain, singing the Beatles, "Good Day Sunshine," helped me move on from the tornado scare. As I backtracked to meet up with the Blue Ridge Threshold Choir in Harrisonburg, Virginia, I couldn't help noticing signs posted every few miles along the route warning, "Speed Limit Enforced by Aircraft." It had been decades since I had seen that particular traffic control sign, and even as a gullible kid, I suspected it was an empty threat. I certainly didn't see any aircraft, and in all my years of driving, I have never seen aircraft patrolling highways. With improvements in technology over the past few decades, I had to wonder if this was the same old bluff, or if Virginia's rural highways are now patrolled by speed detecting aircraft in the form of satellites and drones.

The Benevolent Mennonites

On the drive from Richmond to Harrisonburg, Virginia, I stopped to explore Grand Caverns, a tourist attraction since its discovery in 1806. As our group was led from one elaborate stone draped "room" to the next, the mineral rich smell of wet soil made it hard to forget that we were wandering 200 feet below the surface of the earth. With the long-lasting impact of Mark Twain's account of Tom Sawyer and Becky Thatcher hopelessly lost in just such a cavern, I couldn't peer down the deep crevasses or look at the progressions of dark chambers without feeling a shiver down my spine.

In Harrisonburg, Donna, the Blue Ridge Threshold Choir director, made arrangements for me to overnight in the Mennonite church parking lot. The first thing I noticed were the signs welcoming immigrants, and those of all faiths, posted in the parking lot and in yards around the city.

At the practice, I learned this choir regularly sings to community members well known to them, and they practice hymns that are part of a culture they share. Having sung together for many years in church choirs, the Blue Ridge Threshold Choir sounded like a chorus of angels as they practiced a mix of Threshold Choir repertoire and the hymns that provide comfort within their community.

Our repertoire is primarily spiritual, not religious. Although many choir members are affiliated with faith-based groups and church choirs, the international organization has no such affiliation. TCI greatly benefits from the diversity of members' spiritual paths. In addition to the common repertoire, chapters add original songs and songs that meet the language, cultural, and faith preferences of their members and the communities in which they serve.

Harrisonburg is the home of the Eastern Mennonite University, and the area is the historic home of many different sects of Mennonites, including those in modern dress, like the chapter members I met. One of those members kindly offered to take me on a tour of the Shenandoah Valley. We drove through fertile farmland in the hills around the city where traffic is slowed by traditional horse-drawn buggies. Mennonite subsistence farmers depend on side businesses to support their large families. We visited one of those family businesses that Shirley regularly patronizes, a nursery with acres of greenhouses filled with flowers blooming in a dazzling display of orange, pink, red, yellow, and purple. She brought home some of that spring color for her garden.

With a history of pacifism and conscientious objection dating back to the Civil War, the Mennonites are one of only three religions recognized by the US government as Conscientious Objectors. Shirley was married during the Vietnam Conflict, and within weeks of the wedding, her husband's draft number was called. The US requires foreign service to maintain Conscientious Objector status, and the young newlyweds were sent to Haiti, where Shirley worked as a nurse and her husband held a civil servant job. She remembers their two years in that tropical country as a wonderful time. Years later, when they were called to India for five years of civil service, Shirley was in charge of a support program for mothers and children. She said it was important work that she was honored to do.

I was first introduced to the Mennonites while I was deployed with FEMA in Cedar Rapids, Iowa, following the devastating flood of 2008. Within days of the disaster, they arrived on the scene with tools and building supplies, and proceeded to remove contaminated floors and walls and rebuild them. They offered their services to flood victims who could not afford to hire help, providing an essential service that FEMA, the Red Cross, and insurance companies do not offer.

From Harrisonburg, I followed scenic Skyline Drive to Shenandoah National Park. Forests with the ground littered with fallen trees and branches were signs of the severe weather events I was witnessing. With another storm due in two days, I spent just one memorable night at the National Park campground before seeking a more more sheltered location.

The Appalachian Trail intersects this campground, bringing scores of weary backpackers at the end of day. One of those hikers stopped by my camp to tell me he was on a mission to bring Jesus to the Appalachian Trail. He said I was the eightieth person to receive his "message of truth." His speech threatened a Day of Reckoning, and he voiced his concern that my eternal soul was in deep trouble if I did not accept Jesus as my savior. I explained that although I feel nothing but love for Jesus, the glorification of suffering piece is not for me. I prefer to focus on his message of love. After a lifetime of feeling pain when I see a crucifix, including the one that hung over my parent's bed, I thank Mathew Fox and his book, *Original Blessing,* for helping me understand that response.[43] This God-fearing hiker's truth is not my truth. My concerned visitor made me grateful to be living without the fear of death and damnation, and to have an opportunity to provide service to others that is free of judgment.

Heartbreak at Monticello

In Charlottesville, Virginia, I was invited to park on a charming tree-lined street in front of the home of a choir member. An invitation to join a bedside sing introduced me to the Charlottesville Threshold Singers' ritual of gathering for a moment of silence and setting intention before entering each patient's room.

My hosts, Lynn and Glen, are impressive elders. In addition to the Threshold Choir, Lynn, a retired music teacher, is active in other community activities. She plays racquetball three times a week and leads sing-a-longs at nursing homes. Her husband left for a morning swim each day at 5:30 a.m. Glen also came to my aid repairing the collapsed rod in my tiny overstuffed closet, a job that required more than two hands.

Before leaving this charming city with dogwood and redbud trees in full bloom, I stopped at Thomas Jefferson's Monticello estate. Seeing the beauty of the manicured gardens, unique architecture, and hilltop view was not the uplifting experience one would expect.

To acknowledge the hardships endured by the 169 men, women, and children who were enslaved on the estate, the slave quarters have been reconstructed, and docents educate the public about their lives. Although the knowledge that Jefferson fathered six children with enslaved Sally Hemings is well known, it was devastating to learn the painful truth of the long hours of hard labor, poor living conditions, and lack of food that the enslaved were subjected to by the brilliant man who is revered as a Founding Father of our nation.

The fact that slavery existed in all thirteen colonies at the time the Declaration of Independence was signed, and that many of the delegates to the Constitutional Convention owned enslaved people, as did eight of the first twelve US presidents, certainly calls into question the integrity of the celebrated words "that all men are created equal, that they are endowed by their Creator with certain unalienable rights, that among these are Life, Liberty and the pursuit of Happiness."

As the debate about educating our youth rages, I ask how we will avoid repeating the mistakes of the past if we don't study the truth of our history and recognize the consequences of racism and social injustice. I am grateful that visitors to Monticello have an opportunity to learn about the lives of the enslaved on Jefferson's estate. The truth can guide us in creating a more equitable world.

While making my way towards a choir practice in Washington D.C., I discovered scenic back roads and learned of the rich history of Virginia, West Virginia, and Maryland. In the historic downtowns, brick row houses, similar to the ones I saw in Dublin, intrigued me. The bricks told of 200 years of renovations and add-ons to the two story homes that began as modest single story structures. The durability of the bricks had me thinking about the Three Little Pigs and the safety they found in their house made of bricks when I heard the warning that another swarm of tornadoes was heading my way. I sought refuge in a brick hotel in Winchester, Virginia, while more than a dozen tornadoes touched down in the state.

At the confluence of the celebrated Shenandoah and Potomac Rivers, I stopped to wander around Harper's Ferry National Historic Park, the site of John Brown's failed abolitionist Rebellion in 1859. The little town of Harper's Ferry is also home to Storer College, a progressive institution that functioned primarily as a college for "Colored students" from 1867 to 1955, but also accepted female and white students.

A wrong turn led me to a trail along the Chesapeake and Ohio Canal towpath and, eventually, to the elegant downtown district of Frederick, Maryland. I camped at Greenbelt Park, a wooded haven just outside Washington, D.C. Climbing to the top of an old stone water tower gave me a close-up view of a massive eagle's nest built in the graffitied rafters of the wooden roof.

CHAPTER 12

The Marvel of Nautical Twilight

The Administrative Director of the Threshold Singers of Washington, D.C., invited me to park outside her home, a short distance from the capitol. Leslie was preparing to honor a member's graduation to bedside singing, and we discussed the chapter's process for advancement. Each chapter establishes criteria to determine eligibility for bedside singing. For those joining this chapter, graduation is a celebration that includes sharing feelings about the service and the choir, as well as gifts of a Threshold Choir pin and a small shoulder bag to use for essentials at bedsides.

Although there are singers who join Threshold Choir with the intention of singing only at choir practices and gatherings, most of us are anxious to reach the point where we can provide the service of singing at bedsides. The focus and dedication required of bedside singers is substantial. When I started singing with the choir, Kate Munger told me to expect to spend a year learning the songs, the ability to blend my voice with other singers, bedside protocol, and the meaning of this service. It did take a year before the Aromas Threshold Choir I trained with felt I was ready.

Before taking off for my next choir rendezvous in Philadelphia, Pennsylvania, Leslie and her husband, Don, provided directions and Metro tokens for a day soaking in the magnificence of the National Mall and the National Gallery of Art. I missed the cherry tree bloom by two weeks, but arrived in time to walk through wide swaths of pink petals blanketing the ground beneath the trees.

In Philadelphia, I was honored to be invited to meet with the leadership council of the Philadelphia Threshold Singers prior to the chapter's practice. Planning for the evening practice included addressing a sensitive issue. At a previous practice, a member had raised an objection to singing what she considered to be a religious song. She was not comfortable singing religious songs. The council decided to spend part of the upcoming practice in small break-out groups in which members would share their feelings about singing that song, and other songs requested at practices and at bedsides that might be considered religious, or otherwise make a member uncomfortable.

In the break-out group at the Philadelphia Threshold Singers practice that evening, Lana Noel pointed out that although we want to honor the requests of patients, "We also need to take care of each other." The conscious leadership of this choir was a valuable reminder of the culture of caring that is the heart and soul of Threshold Choir. Many of us find it easy to put patient needs above our own.

Suzanne kindly invited me to park outside her condo in Philadelphia where there was easy access to public transportation to flamboyant downtown Philly. I explored City Center, took in the view from the top floor of One Liberty Place, stood in line to see the Liberty Bell, and ate a cheesesteak sandwich at the bustling Reading Terminal Market.

With a storm moving into the area and the possibility of tornadoes touching down in Philadelphia, I headed north from there, seeking refuge in a hotel room outside of Trenton, New Jersey. An hour before the storm's predicted arrival, I nervously walked across the street to the Quick Stop for dinner supplies. Once again, despite excited meteorologists' warnings, I seemed to be the only one concerned. It was a long night, but damages from the storms and a tornado that landed in Maryland were minimal. I was not forced to sleep in the bathtub with a mattress over my head, as I was prepared to do.

With four days to get to my next scheduled stop in western Massachusetts, I had time to join the Lower Hudson Valley Threshold Singers in New York for a Sunday afternoon practice at a nursing home, followed by bedside singing in the facility. I parked at a choir member's hilltop home. Beth and her husband, Scott, have been singing in elementary schools for thirty years.

Cat led the choir practice. A talented professional vocalist, she brings singing to corporate settings. The ability and confidence level of this group made for an ease and playfulness rarely seen at choir practices. When we visited patient rooms, those who were awake and communicative were asked if they preferred soothing music or something upbeat. We sang the Threshold Choir repertoire we practiced, and more lively songs when requested. Our rendition of "New York, New York," and our attempt at chorus line kicks, elevated the mood of patients and staff alike. This chapter has complied with requests for everything from sea shanties to rap, and I was told that one of the singers responded to a bedside request with something from "Hamilton."

I had been looking forward to a visit with Susan in southern New York State ever since she enthusiastically extended an invitation on the day I announced the journey in 2017. She showed me around her town of Beacon, on the banks of the Hudson, where brick structures that once housed manufacturing have been converted to up-scale shops, restaurants, and the live/work lofts that are much in demand by smart young professionals working in New York City. The beautiful Hudson Valley is Pete Seeger country, and it is heartening to see that his efforts to organize the clean-up of the Hudson River have been fruitful. I was awed by the mighty Hudson and by New York State, which would call me back again.

In Massachusetts, my reunion with Renée, a friend for nearly fifty years, was ecstatic. I was able to retrieve the vehicle registration sticker I needed on the last day the van was legal, a minor miracle considering the problems with fees and address changes that resulted in several back-and-forth letters with the California DMV. I depended on my son, Kel, to keep up with my mail and bills for toll road fees forwarded to his mailing address on the opposite coast. As a moving target, staying on top of personal business is difficult. When I lost a credit card, I had to ask a choir member I hadn't met if the replacement card could be sent ahead to her in a town where I was headed. The help I received from family, friends, and those who would become friends, made it all work.

After an eventful month singing with eight Threshold Choirs, traveling through ten states, sightseeing at three National Parks, and dodging four tornadoes, slowing down to spend a week parked in Renée's Northampton driveway was rejuvenating. Even after all these years, I continue to be amazed by how much Renée and I have in common.

Understanding, as few would, that traveling without my sewing machine was challenging for me, she made hers available during my visit and I constructed a colorful sleeve to protect my all-important laptop computer.

Sing Every Day

From Northampton, my next stop was Salem, and the Threshold Singers of the North Shore, where it was my good fortune that Jane offered her driveway in Marblehead, Massachusetts. The home that belonged to her grandmother is a traditional gambrel roofed gem with a flowering garden and a sweeping view of Salem Bay, even from the driveway. Jane had been singing with Threshold Choir for ten years and was actively assisting the talented music director of the choir. We shared meals, songs, life stories, poetry, art, and went to the choir practice together. Valerie, a retired music teacher, the director of the choir, teaches voice along with Threshold repertoire. The extensive warm-up exercises were especially helpful for me. Talking to Valerie about my struggles with my aging voice, she gave me what may be the most valuable advice I have heard: "Sing every day." Good for the spirit as well as the voice.

Fast asleep in Jane's driveway, I was awakened at 4:40 a.m. by a magenta horizon and soft light reflected on the quiet water. It didn't make sense; sunrise at latitude 42.50° N was still an hour away. What was going on? Research online revealed that I was observing Nautical Twilight, an occurrence that began at 4:38 on this sixth day of May. Nautical Twilight is defined as a time before sunrise or sunset when both the horizon and brighter stars are visible, making it possible to navigate at sea. How fitting to be introduced to this mysterious morning light here, where all things nautical apply, and where the survival of seafarers has long depended on the ability to safely navigate this wickedly rocky coastline.

Saying goodbye to Jane, I felt that familiar mix of joy for the meaningful connection, and sadness knowing our paths may not cross again, a sign I had encountered a kindred spirit.

With a week before I would join a practice of the Rhode Island chapter, I detoured to Maine. Campgrounds would not open for another month, no overnights were permitted in rest stops, and Cracker Barrel parking lots disappeared as I traveled north, finding a place to safely park at night was getting harder. Choir members' driveways offered security and respite, but there were no Threshold Choir chapters where I was headed.

A Harvest Host membership solved my dilemma. The subscription phone app offers RV travelers overnight parking at participating breweries, wineries, and farms. In Portsmouth, New Hampshire, my first Harvest Host night was spent in the parking lot of the Cisco Brewery, where music, food, and a spectacular Irish Guinness-style creamy stout waited. Harvest Host offered safe havens for the remainder of the trip.

Donuts, Lobster Rolls, and Whoopie Pies

Traveling the coast of Main off-season has advantages and disadvantages. In the lobster fishing port, Boothbay, it was too early for puffin cruises, kayak rentals, and ferry boats, but a Harvest Host brewery offered friendly companionship, pub songs, and a place to park for the night. The deep water coves, inlets, and bays along this jagged stretch of coastline were stacked high with lobster traps primed for the Memorial Day start of the season locals call Spring.

Even in the off-season, fresh lobster is available here, and I couldn't visit Maine without trying the area's most famous offering, a lobster roll. I placed my order at the weather-worn lobster shack on a waterfront wharf, where the $28.00 bill for the sandwich caught me off guard. The "roll" is actually a thick slice of white bread split open and stuffed with, in this case anyway, one-and-a-half pounds of deliciously fresh lobster meat with a bit of melted butter, honest and unadulterated. I ate lobster leftovers for two days.

It wasn't hard to figure out that donuts and whoopie pies are close runners-up to lobster as favorite foods in this part of the world. In the sleepy beach town of Ogunquit, Congdon's Donut Shop was buzzing with activity. Seeing the parking lot and the overflow parking nearly full was a tip-off that I had stumbled upon a culinary hot spot. It was 11:00 a.m. when I entered the bustling diner where whoopie pies in sizes ranging from Oreo cookie to birthday cake lined shining glass cabinets. With the help of six young employees working at lightning speed, donuts were flying off the shelves. Many shelves were empty at this point, including, sadly, the apple fritters shelf. I settled for an egg benedict sandwich for $3.50, a deal at any price.

Reluctant to leave Maine, I stopped in the tourist haven, Kennebunkport. It was not off-season there, and traffic moved at a crawl in the narrow streets of this quaint seaport. This was the place to be on this sunny Mother's Day. The line at the Clam Shack stretched a block long, cafés were bustling, and there were plenty of upscale shops and galleries to peruse. In one alluring storefront window, a "Sale" sign on a pair of crazy striped rubber booties caught my eye. Just the thing for stylish camping in the muck, I couldn't resist adding them to the stash of shoes and hats that dominated my tiny living space.

Physical Limitations

Camilla offered her driveway for my visit to the Grace Note Singers (now the Providence Threshold Singers) in Providence, Rhode Island. She and her husband, Mike, did a custom build on their own camper van and they had a wealth of valuable camping tips to pass along, including washing dishes with one cup of water. Although I never quite mastered the one-cup wash method, I think of Camilla often as I use the squeeze bottle designed for hair dye that she recommended for dispensing dish soap by the drop. Saving soap, and consequently, rinse water, with my little squeeze bottle led to nearly a year of dishwashing from one twenty-four ounce bottle of dish soap. Eliminating waste suits my newly found joy of living a minimalist lifestyle.

In addition to possessing superior camping skills, Camilla sings in other choirs, and is a musician long committed to a contra dancing community. At a monthly contra dancing shindig she invited me to join, I was reminded why I had to quit West Coast Swing dancing. The spinning and turns made me dizzy. To avoid feeling seasick, I had to sit out the evening watching the fun and listening to the music. I can't deny feeling a bit sorry for myself seeing other white-haired folks happily spinning away on the dance floor while I was forced to remain grounded. Yay for those who continue dancing and spinning while they can!

Joining the Grace Note Singers practice, I appreciated the innovation of this chapter and its forty-five plus singers. Years before, a decision was made that the choir would be led by committee, with each member asked to choose a committee in which they would participate. The members of the music committee led warm-ups and songs at the practice, and I was invited to join a bedside sing afterward. Before the singers entered a hospital room, a "point person" checked in with patients and their families, asking them to honor the silence between songs, and letting patients know that falling asleep during the singing is strongly encouraged.

After an action-packed stay in Rhode Island, I headed back to Massachusetts with a request to join the Threshold Singers of Indian Hill Music in Littleton. Their practices are held at a music center that offers the space for no charge because the mission of Threshold Choir is closely aligned with the center's mission to serve their community. During the practice, the members were asked to take turns telling what it means to them to sing with the choir. As with the other chapters I have visited, the themes of gratitude, service, purpose and belonging were the sentiments voiced. The music director, Charlotte, is a professional voice teacher who offers a third practice each month for help with voice and technique. She said it is important to work on technique to create a sound that is soothing at bedsides.

Questioning Worthiness

Difficulties locating a place to park overnight in Littleton had me questioning my worthiness. As a stranger to most choir members when I arrive, doubts about whether I'm asking too much of those I visit, and whether my travels are purely self-serving, are demons that surface at times. I know that my uninvited visit can be a disruption. Every precious minute of a Threshold Choir practice is devoted to singing in small groups, preparing songs, learning harmonies, attending to choir business, and sharing recent bedside experiences. I don't bring an impressive voice or songs I have written. I can't sing all the harmony parts or offer the musicianship that others can bring to the table.

There were times when I drove for hours searching for a safe spot to overnight because I just couldn't bring myself to ask another choir member I hadn't met for overnight parking. After decades of occupying my time with service in my community, this journey required a major shift. Advice from a wise and wonderful elder and Threshold Choir leader, Marilyn Power Scott, "We have a time in our lives for giving and a time for receiving," was reassuring, but guilt-free receiving doesn't come easily for this fiercely independent woman.

In clearer moments, I know that the visits I made to choirs have worth. By showing up, it was my intention to acknowledge and honor choir members and what they do, to let them know they are seen. I have deep respect and admiration for the efforts made by Threshold Choir chapters, directors, and singers, how they support each other, and the way they work together toward the goal of bringing compassion and beauty to bedsides. Perhaps it is rationalization on my part, but I would like to think my visits also provide an example for others who might need a nudge to pursue their own wild dreams.

In the midst of a circle of bedside singers, like the practice I joined at the Indian Hill Music Center, my doubts vanish. I can feel the river of love that connects us in this service. I am home.

In the Kitchen with Dinah, Yellow Springs, OH.

CHAPTER 13

Her Grandmother's Biscuits

The alarming noise in the front end of the Roadtrek flared up again on a lonely stretch of highway in the countryside of New York State heading into the Catskills. With no repair shop in the vicinity, I followed the directions on my Allstays app to an RV repair shop sixty miles away. They referred me to a truck repair shop on Sawkill Ruby Road.

Personable Mike immediately put one of his mechanics on the job, pulling him off other work in the busy shop. After a series of expensive repairs, this was the point when I stopped counting. I admitted to myself that no matter the cost of the repair, I was committed to this journey. As long as I kept throwing money at her, Wanda would take me wherever I needed to go. This insight, along with a generous donation from my brother, who happened to call while I was in the shop waiting for the repair to be completed, helped me reclaim my traveling groove.

The drive to my campsite that evening wound through a paradise of rushing rivers, carved stone gorges, and cascading waterfalls. At the end of a long day, I arrived at the North-South Lake Campground, and the beauty was astounding. Among clear running streams and beaver downed trees, I found a campsite on the lake. A sign told of the history of the place: the lake and the surrounding mountains were made famous in the 1800s by Thomas Cole and the gifted landscape artists of the Hudson River School. Waking at the water's edge the next morning, I enjoyed a perfect cup of coffee while gazing at the shining lake framed by serene mountain peaks. I was in the midst one of those revered paintings.

From the wilds of the Catskills, I traveled back roads in southeastern New York, stopping more than once for Canada geese leading a line of fluffy goslings across the road with great authority. Twenty minutes from my next campground stop, I turned off the main road to the village of Cazenovia. I wasn't ready to settle in for another long night without human contact.

In the soft light of a fading spring day, I walked past the town's white steepled churches, the brownstone buildings of a small private college, and grand homes with acres of expansive, unfenced lawns and flowering trees. Just when I was looking for a good reason to stick around, a sign in the window of a restaurant advertised happy hour and a $10.00 pasta special.

Inside the restaurant, I became aware that the small group of ponytailed men and well-dressed women at the end of the bar shared my anxiety about the political state of the country. I let them know how happy I was to hear I was not alone feeling those concerns, which has not always been the case in my travels. As it turned out, they were musicians interested in my song-driven journey. They asked how I stumbled upon their idyllic hamlet as if it were a well-kept secret, and I felt like a bonafide traveler answering, "The road led me."

On the road to my campsite at Green Lakes State Park, curiously, I started singing, "Fifteen Miles on the Erie Canal." This is one of the tunes indelibly etched on my mind since grade school. I was belting out the words that I was surprised I knew after so many years, when I came to a bridge and a sign, "Old Erie Canal State Park." The song knew where I was before I could figure it out.

Arriving ahead of Memorial Day weekend crowds, I was able to enjoy the forests and jewel-like meromictic lakes of Green Lakes State Park in peaceful quiet before heading to Niagara Falls. This was my first time to see the falls. My entire body reacted to the riveting power of the water racing to the tremendous drop and the force of the 180-foot fall that transforms the water to a fine mist. From Niagara, I continued south to Cleveland along the shore of Lake Erie.

A night at 150-year-old South Shore Wine Company was my first exposure to the largest wine growing region east of the Rocky Mountains. Having once lived in the Sonoma Wine Country, it is a stretch for me to believe grape vines can survive icy northern winters. Thanks to my Harvest Host membership, I wasn't charged for wine tasting or overnight parking. I found the wines offered complex, with just the right balance of fruity sweetness.

Good Times in Cleveland

I had been looking forward to seeing Wendy in Cleveland ever since we struck up a new friendship at the gathering in Boulder in June of 2018, but I had no idea the visit would be so much fun. Wendy's kind welcome included a delicious dinner and a healing massage. For real. She was studying to become a Certified Music Therapist. Her husband, Ron, a professor and cultural anthropologist, shared fascinating tales and artifacts from his years living in Ethiopia.

My hosts kindly took me to see all the sights in the area. We walked among the azaleas in the arboretum and fluttering butterflies in the glasshouse of the Cleveland Botanical Garden, visited the space-age geodesic dome structure at the American Society for Metals, spent an evening at the Cleveland Museum of Art, and explored their charming village with the unfortunate name, Chagrin Falls.

At the Threshold Choir of Cleveland practice, choir members who had been following my blog talked to me about my adventures. They practice in a meeting room at a large, multi-level care facility, and at this particular practice, one of the residents wandered in, took a seat at the table and began singing with us. About fifteen minutes after she joined us, our rather confused guest left her chair and started rummaging through the ice chest with treats Wendy brought for a party she planned following the practice. Wendy gently directed the guest back to the table, where she sang with us for the duration.

The practice included a "wander" that started with singing a round while seated at the table, and once we had it, we walked around the room singing to each other. Looking into each other's eyes while singing in close proximity makes for a very personal connection, and it builds skill and confidence to hold your part while face to face with someone singing another part.

Asking members to share one or two words that describe why they participate in Threshold Choir has been a bonding experience for this chapter. It was explained to me that in Cleveland, attending choir practices can mean driving through snow, sleet, and hail. Members asked to complete the statement, "I come to Threshold Choir because of..." came up with this list of answers: *service, community, comfort, grace, connection, humility, empathy, humbleness, the ineffable, sacred space, anam cara (soul friend), calling, ministry, mutual exchange, honor.* I would add to this list, *the songs.* After the practice, the party Wendy rolled out in honor of my visit included berry pie, gifts, a card created and signed by the members, and a gas contribution. Feeling the love.

The Right Place at the Right Time

Venturing deeper into tornado country in June made me uneasy, but I made the drive south from Cleveland to Yellow Springs, Ohio, to meet with the chapter I had heard so much about. In the fall of 2019, the Threshold Singers of Yellow Springs would invite Threshold Choirs from the area to attend their fourteenth Annual Regional Gathering. I would be far away by that time; this was my only chance to sing with this well-respected choir.

The charming village that is the home of progressive Antioch College is a picturesque hippie-flavored town, and Dinah's gracious southern hospitality made me feel right at home. Her husband, David, directed me to park in their tree-shaded driveway behind a pock-marked Subaru station wagon. I would learn the car had been damaged by golf ball-sized hail when a tornado passed nearby less than a week before I arrived.

Elegant Dinah extended a warm invitation to dinner, and David took us out for sight-seeing and ice cream afterward. I felt like a kid visiting my favorite aunt and uncle. Within moments of my arrival, I was invited to join her and another member of the Threshold Singers of Yellow Springs at a bedside the next morning to sing for a patient whose time was close. The singing request came from a Threshold Choir member from California, who was in Ohio to be with her dying mother. It was an honor to be included, especially considering that Dinah and I had never sung together. She gave me the song list she had prepared, and I reviewed the soprano harmonies I would contribute to the group. The miracle of our shared repertoire makes stepping in at bedsides possible.

The three of us started out early, with plans to meet Mary in the parking lot of the facility at 9:00 a.m. The drive took over an hour. I'm certain Dinah, who is a fountain of kindness and commitment, would have agreed to drive many times that distance to help another choir member, or anyone in need. When we arrived, Mary and I recognized each other from the RiverSong Threshold Choir practice I attended in California six months earlier, adding a layer of shared history to the bond all choir members feel. I took this as validation I was exactly where I was supposed to be, exactly when I was supposed to be there.

After she led us into the facility where family members gathered in vigil around her mother, Mary told them about our connection. As we often find when family gathers at the bedside of one whose time is close, the room was charged with love. Mary's lovely voice and the devotion she showed her mother as she stroked her hair and face added depth and meaning to this beautiful bedside sing. Her mother's eyes were closed while we sang, and the uncomfortable fidgeting she exhibited at the start slowly calmed. All present at the bedside were lifted.

The practice of the Threshold Singers of Yellow

Springs I attended fell within a week of the Memorial Day tornado that touched down close to a choir member's home in nearby Dayton. The near miss triggered trauma from the devastation caused by past tornadoes. Telling us she had been counting the days until the practice, this cherished choir member explained that the promise of receiving time in the chair kept her going through the difficult week following the tornado. Invited to spend as much time as she needed in the chair in the center of the circle, she was lovingly showered with song for the entire practice. She told us the time she spent being sung to in the chair was the only calm she had felt in the six days since the tornado ripped through the area.

Among the kindnesses received from choir members, Dinah's light and flaky homemade biscuits made a lasting impression. Using her grandmother's recipe and white enameled mixing bowl, Dinah whipped up the biscuits as part of the hearty breakfasts of eggs, ham, gravy, and larrup (stewed berries for spooning over biscuits) she prepared during my stay. On the morning I was leaving for my next choir stop, she handed me a card on which she had written her grandmother's precious biscuit recipe. The gift was a touching reminder that we are all part of what Melanie DeMore calls "the global family that Kate created."

On to Ann Arbor, Michigan, where I looked forward to staying in the driveway of my friend, Tammy, the founder of the Threshold Singers of Ann Arbor. We share a mutual friendship with Renée in Massachusetts, and Tammy stayed with me in Pacific Grove when she attended a Threshold Choir gathering in California.

One of the scores of leaders who, like myself, received support from Kate to start chapters in their communities, Tammy told me she started the Threshold Singers of Ann Arbor one month after meeting Kate at the 2007 Regional Gathering in Yellow Springs. With the first song, Tammy knew this was exactly what she had been looking for since witnessing her mother's death and the comfort singing at her bedside provided. At her mother's request, Tammy made sure she heard non-stop music during her last week of life, playing recorded music when she wasn't singing or playing piano for her. After seeing how the music relaxed her mother, helped her breathing and eased her transition, Tammy felt the calling.

The Ann Arbor practice was rich with beautiful song and consideration for each other's needs. Susie's calm and compassionate direction of the practice provided the support members needed to express their feelings as we moved into a sensitive discussion about a member's sudden announcement that she was leaving the choir. Sadness and concern were expressed regarding her choice to leave because she felt frustrated and inadequate after her efforts had not yet resulted in graduation to bedside singing. A thoughtful discussion following the announcement resulted in a decision to review and update the choir's current requirements to become a bedside singer.

After some singing that included my Threshold Choir contribution, "Duerme," and original songs written by the talented members of this choir, the practice moved to a discussion on diversity. Edie, a talented diversity trainer and member of the choir, skillfully led the brief training. Her suggestions to practice "awareness, compassion, and action," and to always consider the consequences of our actions, are valuable tools.

In Praise of Spontaneity

I hadn't decided which direction I would travel when I left Ann Arbor. Originally, I planned to start heading west toward the Rockies after Michigan, stopping in Chicago along the way. After the Memorial Day tornado in Ohio, and the other near misses, crossing the Midwest during the month of June, a productive tornado month, did not seem like the best idea. An unscheduled right turn as I left Tammy's house had me heading eastward instead.

In that moment, I decided I would spend the rest of June in the Catskill Mountains in New York, where I hoped to be safe from tornadoes, and I could join Lisa G. Littlebird for a singing retreat at the Omega Institute. The choice would mean I had a great distance to travel. Another fateful turn sent me across the Canadian border where I followed the north shore of Lake Ontario east. I had already traveled the southern route, indulging my curiosity, I would travel territory that was new to me.

At the Visitor Center in London, Ontario, I stopped for a much-needed break. I snacked on cheese, crackers, and juicy red grapes before walking a nature trail. On the boardwalk that wound through wetlands and around ponds covered with lilies, I amused myself calling to bullfrogs using a clucking technique demonstrated by Ron in Cleveland. Making use of the Visitor Center's internet to look for Threshold Choirs in the area, I was pleased to discover the London Ontario Threshold Choir would be practicing nearby in two hours.

I was invited to join the practice and Elaine offered her guest room for the night. The year-old choir sounded gorgeous, and thanks to Elaine's skilled direction, they were already offering singing at bedsides and hospice events. That night, we stayed up late swapping personal stories and talking about the chapter's process of welcoming new members, supporting members who aren't able to match pitch, blend, or sing softly, and the difficult task of lovingly letting members know if it isn't working out. I shared my discomfort turning away a musician friend with a booming Broadway musical style, who could not modulate the volume of his voice to blend with the other singers. Concerned that our friendship would be damaged, I discovered that being totally honest from the beginning was an approach that helped both of us.

It was a little slice of heaven to stay with Elaine in her resort-like home and join her for a morning swim in her pool before hitting the road. Spontaneity paid off.

Crossing back to upstate New York, I spent the next three days exploring the countryside before returning to the Catskills for six nights at Lake Taghkanic State Park, my longest campground stay so far. I needed a break from driving and from the task of figuring out where to sleep next.

During those stretches of solitude between visits to Threshold Choirs, friends, and family, I had very little interaction with others outside of the customary nod or wave campers extend to each other in passing. I passed many "days without words," immersed in the nourishing silence my friend, Marj Davis, embraces. With phone service available only about half of the time, the few phone calls I made were primarily to arrange for choir stops, and I often found myself procrastinating about making those calls. I could have called friends and family more often, but I was so fully engaged with the world around me and within me, that it rarely occurred to me.

Even in the spectacular setting of Lake Taghkanic State Park, after days without human interaction, that familiar longing filled me. In *Anam Cara*, John O'Donohue wrote that being born into a human body creates a separation from others that drives us to spend a lifetime seeking connection. Joining Lisa G. for days of interactive singing at the Omega Institute for Holistic Studies was certain to fulfill the longing I was feeling for meaningful connection.

From Days Without Words ### *to Days Filled with Song*

Lisa G. Littlebird defines community singing as "socially acceptable intimacy," and that is exactly what was on the menu at the *Singing Our Way Back Together* retreat where I joined Lisa, my close friend, Pacia, and twelve others. Lisa and Lyndsey Scott, the gifted co-leaders of the gathering, provided opportunities for the kind of shared joy, laughter, and tears that break through the barriers that separate us.

Lisa is skilled at sharing songs that speak to the heart, and one of her song choices moved me to tears. A favorite for bedside sings, "Navajo Prayer," brought back years of Threshold singing with Jill and Suzan. I was overcome with emotion realizing how much I missed my choir sisters and the regular bedside singing we did together. I had a deep cry. It was the kind of homesick sobbing I remember from summer camp as a little kid.

On one hospice sing, we added "Navajo Prayer" to our "setlist" for a patient because Jill told us she woke up singing the song, and it had stayed with her all day asking to be sung. Softly repeating the rhythmic message to the unresponsive patient that evening, we noticed that family members holding vigil in her hospital room were overcome with emotion. They told us how fitting the words of the song were on this day, which happened to be their loved one's birthday, and, we learned later, the day she died.

Navajo Prayer
©2004 Jody Healy

When you were born, you cried
And the world rejoiced.
Live your life so that when you die
The world cries and you rejoice.

Lisa tells us it is the unfiltered authenticity of singing that clears the way for emotion and connection. She also reminds us that when we sing, we are not only connecting with those singing in the room with us, "we are connected with anyone who has ever sung that song." She encourages "trying on songs from other cultures to awaken deeper capacities within ourselves." Acknowledging historical, spiritual, and cultural significance of the songs she shares, Lisa stresses sensitivity to cultural appropriation.

Also a devoted racial and social justice activist,

Lyndsey told me she prays to be worthy to carry the songs she is passionate about. For her, "singing African American spirituals and the South African songs that called for freedom from apartheid opens channels of longing." It is her feeling that singing those songs, we participate in the "realization of a shared dream."

Song was a portal to just such a shared dream when I stood within the stone ruins of a 1,500-year-old church on Holy Island in Lough Derg, Ireland, while Nóirín Ni Riain, and her sons, Micheál and Owen Ó Súilleabháin, sang Gregorian chants. Time ceased to exist as sacred songs resonating in the ancient chapel linked us to the past of the island and to the monks who once sang those eternal chants here.

A song written by Melanie DeMore showed up at one of the ancient sites I had the privilege to visit in Ireland. When the group of musicians, poets, and spiritual leaders I traveled with visited Grange Circle, the oldest circle of standing stones in Ireland, we were encouraged to touch the stones. In the prehistoric circle, one can feel the energy held by the stones and the presence of all who have drawn inspiration from them.

Lying in stillness on the hallowed ground within the circle, the song, "Standing Stone," surfaced. In the lyrics, I heard the voices of the stones, those whose labor transported them to this location to create this holy place, and the many generations of devotees who have come to know the blessing of the stones. The powerful message that brings such comfort at bedsides expanded in depth and meaning when sung to honor this circle of standing stones in far-off Ireland.

Standing Stone
by Melanie DeMore

I will be your standing stone.
I will stand by you.

Grandeur

With a full heart, I left singing summer camp feeling the need for time alone to process and write. The contemplative quiet I sought was not to be found in the midst of the all-night partying taking place in the parking lot of the 24 hour Walmart where I spent the next night.

In the days that followed, I explored the gorgeous Hudson River Valley with a drive-by of the prestigious Culinary Institute and a walk down a street of well-appointed shop windows in the village of Rhinebeck. As in other up-scale towns I visited in New York, displays of the airy rainbow sherbet hued linen clothing this sultry summer weather begged for tested my resolve not to add to the excessive wardrobe I lugged around. At Vassar College, I wandered the manicured campus of one of the nation's first women's colleges, walking in the esteemed foot-steps of Edna St. Vincent Millay, Jane Fonda, and my Aunt Connie.

In Albany, the New York State Capitol building took my breath away. It is as grand as any European castle, and the palatial Delaware and Hudson Railroad Company complex, nearby, is a Gothic masterpiece. Downgrading from the grandeur of the Empire State Plaza to another Cracker Barrel parking lot night, I slowly made my way back to Massachusetts for one more visit with Renée before my mission would carry me far from the area.

CHAPTER 14

Where Trust Leads

It was a long haul to Erie, Pennsylvania, for my next choir practice, and rain slowed my progress. Exhausted after hours of challenging driving, I stopped for a pick-me-up chocolate milkshake at a fast-food restaurant one afternoon when the sky suddenly darkened. My phone confirmed that a thunderstorm was about to pass through, and I managed to get back to the van and move to a more sheltered location before the rain started. Once settled, I could relax and observe what I now recognize as the pattern of a thundershower: a fickle wind, sideways rain, flashes of lightning, and rumbling thunder followed by intermittent downpours.

Stretching out on my little bed surrounded by windows, I watched, pleased to have an opportunity to be still and give the spectacle my full attention. The sound of the rain pounding the van (and washing it, thank you very much) shut out any other thoughts as I watched the storm build, crescendo, and pass. The marvelous matinee would be repeated many times over the summer. Because I replaced the twenty-year-old rubber gaskets around the skylights and windows when I was in Florida, I could observe cloudbursts from my cozy weathertight capsule without concern for leaking.

Tattoos

After a couple more Cracker Barrel nights, I arrived in Erie and was invited to park at the home of the director of the Great Lakes Erie Threshold Choir. Linda launched this chapter in 2013 after attending a Regional Gathering in Yellow Springs. One has to wonder just how many chapters credit the annual gatherings produced by the dedicated members of the Threshold Singers of Yellow Springs for their start.

The Family Hospice of the University of Pennsylvania Medical Center (UPMC) recognizes bedside singing as a valuable service to clients. They offer support that includes weekly practice space and funding for music, rack cards, bookmarks, and educational materials.

While singing to a choir member in the reclining chair, one of the chapter's bedside anchors had a valuable message for patients who struggle to stay awake while we sing; she told the person in the chair that we consider it a compliment if you fall asleep while we are singing to you. They also use the term, "musical blanket," to describe singing to someone in the reclining chair.

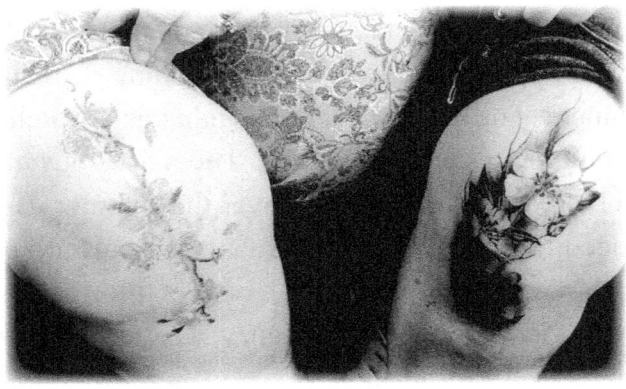

Surgery Scar Adornment.

A highpoint of the evening occurred when two choir members were encouraged to pull up their pant legs to show off their tattoos. Graceful sprays of blossoms adorned the scars of the knee replacement surgery each had undergone.

Erie is a summer playground, and Linda kindly took the time to show me the sights. We visited the beautiful beaches of Presque Isle Park, the harbor, and the glass-walled lakefront library. Like many choir members I visited, Linda is a Master Gardener, and we went on a garden tour with a stop at a friend's enchanting wonderland garden that has been twenty years in the making. On the way home, we stopped for fresh-caught walleye at a restaurant with a view of the sun setting over the lake.

Talking to Angels

From Erie, I spent a night in Cleveland before traveling to Perrysburg, Ohio, home of the Hospice of Northwest Ohio Threshold Choir, and my kind driveway host, Amey. Perrysburg is a charming, and apparently very patriotic, small town on the Maumee River that celebrated the upcoming Fourth of July holiday with a proud display of large American flags, flag bunting, and American flag spinners at nearly every business and home. Amey and I enjoyed tasty pork and mango tacos and illuminating conversation in a Mexican restaurant the night before the practice.

With eighteen years of experience as a hospice nurse, Amey Raihala has fascinating end-of-life stories to tell. She spoke of the agitation and confusion that is followed by calm when someone is close, and explained that "patients on their journey talk about early memories first, and as the transition is progressing, memories come closer to the present." I asked her about patients seeing someone in the room who is not visible to others, an experience our chapter had while singing to a hospice patient who was close to her time. As we sang "Mojuba," a powerful song of the Yoruba people in Nigeria that calls on the ancestors to show us the way, the woman surprised us by looking around the room and telling us, "You girls brought such beautiful people with you."

Amey confirmed that visitors seen only by the dying are common when death is close. If patients ask, she is honest with them, telling them she cannot see the visitor. She asks them to describe what their visitors look like and what it means that they have come. She said sometimes the unseen visitors, or some might say angels, are departed loved ones and sometimes they are persons not known to them.

The choir practice at the Hospice of Northwest Ohio facility was followed by singing patriotic songs at patients' bedsides in honor of the Fourth of July. Not qualified as a volunteer at this hospice, I stood outside in the hallway observing the participatory bedside singing. I was assured by the members that weekly bedside singing at this facility is usually less exuberant. I was deeply touched by a thoughtful gift bag from one of the members; a reusable bag filled with chocolate, sports bars, and bottles of water couldn't have been more fitting for this traveler.

The next evening, I joined locals on the riverbank for the municipal fireworks display, a rare treat for a visitor from fire-traumatized California where fireworks have long been banned. Lightning, thunder, and dancing fireflies augmented the entertainment.

After Perrysburg, I found myself on the shore of Lake Michigan, in Michigan City, Indiana, where a casino parking lot offered overnight parking. The beach scene was in full swing on this holiday weekend with a volleyball tournament, boaters, and a crowded beach that could have been Santa Cruz, only the water was warmer.

When I reached downtown Chicago, I was astonished by Cloud Gate, aka, "The Bean," a massive art installation in Millennium Park. Its shiny metal surface and graceful curves give an interactive fun-house mirror spin to reflections of the sky, the Chicago skyline, and people walking by. An afternoon at the Chicago Institute of Art in the presence of dreamy images created by Gaugin, Chagall, Georgia O'Keeffe, Monet, Manet, and Miro left me feeling giddy.

May Peace Be With You

I traveled to Chicago knowing the Rainbow Threshold Choir had a hospice sing scheduled that I was not qualified to join. This did not stop me from accepting the offer to driveway camp at a member's home north of the city, and to meet with my driveway host, Kathryn, and the director of the choir, Kitty, for lunch. While we were eating, Kitty received a call that her brother was being admitted to the hospital and was not expected to make it. Moments later, she got the call that he had passed.

We listened while Kitty told us about her brother's troubled life. Hearing the stories, Annie Garretson's song, "May Peace Be With You," came forth. Kathryn joined in, and right there in Panera Bread, we quietly sang for Kitty and her brother. Kitty was soon singing with us, and together, we could feel the mood shift from despair to gratitude for an end to her brother's suffering. As happens so frequently, a song with just the right message surfaced when it was needed.

May Peace Be With You
© 2015 by Annie Garretson

May peace be with you.
Peace be with you now.
May peace be with you always.
Peace be with you now and always.

By mid-July, it was hot, road-buckling hot in fact. Sponge baths just don't cut it when you're sweating from every pore. Sticking close to the Great Lakes, I found that even in cities like Chicago, there were beaches where I could take an afternoon swim and wash off that annoying all-over stickiness. No matter how hot the weather, or how warm the lake might be, the outdoor showers at those beaches were surprisingly cold and refreshing.

West of Chicago, I was welcomed by the Threshold Singers of Wheaton, Illinois, the final stop before venturing north. This exceptional choir transitioned to shared leadership after their long-time director stepped down from her leadership role. Kelley, who led the practice I attended, initiated an interesting discussion about the process of choosing songs for patients we know little or nothing about. We talked about cultivating awareness by reading physical clues in the room, such as keepsakes and photos, and observing how clients respond to songs. The intuitive piece, something we very much depend on to guide us in bedside singing, is a divine mystery that is harder to define and to teach.

My driveway host in Wheaton, an energetic retired teacher, was like so many of the choir members I met, a champion of liberal politics in a sea of steadfast conservatism. I honored Sue's request not to mention politics when we dined with her neighbors and good friends of forty years. In these tumultuous times when there is no common language that offers a path to discuss political views, it requires finesse to maintain close relationships with friends and family who have ideologies promoted by different media sources. I have heard over and over again that those subjects must be avoided to keep the peace.

Traveling outside of my progressive California bubble, it was my intention to invite discussion, ask questions, listen, and learn about other perspectives. I had hoped that listening to each other could break down barriers that separate us. In practice, outside of the like-minded world of Threshold Choirs in which I traveled, I was drawn to other progressives with whom I felt safe talking about politics. The subject is so inflammatory that I had not yet found the courage to open that dialogue, but I had hope, and many conservative leaning states ahead.

Driving north through a sea of green corn and soybean fields in northern Illinois and southern Wisconsin had a soothing effect. On stretches where land is not cultivated, tangles of grasses and wildflowers compete for sunlight in an excited frenzy that results in some of those robust weeds reaching heights of over six feet tall. The growing season is short here, and just as plant life bursts forth to soak in seasonal sunshine, the human inhabitants of this northern land come to the area's lakes and rivers to play in the summer sun.

Singing with the Threshold Singers of Chippewa Valley in Eau Claire, Wisconsin, was an honor. This dedicated choir sings at ninety to one hundred bedsides each month. Now that their expansive repertoire is too big and heavy to carry around, members use Kindles for their music. Denise, the director of the choir, invited me to stay in the driveway of her home in the countryside a few miles from town.

Denise and I share a passion for kayaking and canoeing. She told me about the epic summer canoe trips she has taken in the Boundary Waters of northeastern Minnesota for more than forty years. During winter months, this superwoman clears trails for skiing in the woods on her property and chops the wood she clears to heat her home. She did confide that she had recently purchased a gas-operated log splitter to make wood-chopping a bit easier.

Thirty minutes from Eau Claire, I stayed with the Menomonie Threshold Singers' director, Nita, and her husband, Tim. Everything about this chapter felt relaxed and easy. The charming town is built on a lovely lake, and the library where Tim is the reference librarian overlooks the water. Tim and Nita get around on a well-developed bike trail that circles the lake and can take you anywhere you want to go in Menomonie.

At the Farmer's Market, all of the sellers were Hmong people from Laos. Their produce was displayed in tidy baskets, with each vendor's table arranged exactly the same as the others. Someone who saw my license plates asked where I was from in California. Don, who appeared to be in his 90s, had grown up surfing in California and had lived in the canals of Venice Beach where Joe and

I lived in the 1970s before moving to Maui. Those wild and wonderful Venice days were rich with community, beaching, sailing, and rubber rafting in the canals. The unique eight blocks of canals are all that remains of the miraculous canal city constructed in 1905. Having an opportunity to reminisce about the Venice Canals with a stranger in Wisconsin brightened my day.

Dump Station Snub

I explored and camped in Wisconsin and neighboring Minnesota while I waited to join a practice of the Morningstar Singers in Minneapolis. Although I passed other campers on the road, most traveled in big expensive rigs, preferring the electric hookups and TV connections only found in RV Parks. In their eyes, I was still a little hippie girl in a VW van flashing a peace sign. Just how alone I was in the world of RV travel was evident each time I emptied the holding tanks at RV dump stations. Although I saw plenty of travelers at those sites, and often had to wait my turn behind a line of RVs, I was ever the outsider in this exclusively male territory. Women did not venture out of their campers while the dirty work of emptying the sewer waste was performed by the man with whom they traveled.

The one and only time I saw women engaged in the chore was in Wisconsin's Willow Creek State Park, where I was third in the dump line behind two RVs, each with a woman at the helm. Feeling camaraderie, and anxious to know more about these dump station divas, I hopped out of my van to greet them. When I expressed my delight at finding other women dumping, and told them what a pleasure it was to meet women camping alone, I got a cold reception. One of the women snapped at me, saying she wasn't camping alone, as if I had insulted her. She told me she was camping with her mother, and that they traveled in separate RVs because their dogs don't get along. When I told them that during ten months of traveling, I had only seen men performing this duty, the feisty mom quipped, "Oh, I can handle emptying the tank. It's a lot less trouble than putting up with a man."

Beyond Threshold Choir

When I arrived at a practice of the Morningstar Singers in Minneapolis, I was stunned by how similar it was to a Threshold Choir practice. The repertoire, the blending of voices and the reverent silence maintained before moving on to the next song were all familiar. Members also shared recent bedside singing experiences, and the discussion of a memory care patient's response to familiar songs echoed discussions I was hearing at many of the Threshold Choir practices I visited.

Barbara McAfee started Morningstar in 2007 after singing for dying friends and family members; the same inspiration that motivated Kate Munger to start Threshold Choir. Instead of using written music, the Morningstar Singers learn songs orally and add their own harmonies.

On the afternoon I visited, thirty singers sat in easy silence until someone started the next song. Many of their songs were familiar to me, but "Owl Moon," one of this choir's favorites, was a delightful surprise. After the practice, I told Bruce O'Brien how much I liked his sweet song, and learned that he is a member of the Children's

Music Network, where he sang with Kate Munger, and Beth, who I visited in New York. Bruce gave me a CD so I could continue listening while I traveled.

Although it is not possible to know how many of us might be providing the service of singing to those struggling with life and death, I know it is a movement that is growing. Kathy Leo's book, *On the Breath of Song*,[44] describes the radiant spirit of the work and the bedside singing service provided by the Hallowell Singers in Vermont. It is encouraging to know that this mission of compassion is not limited to Threshold Choir singers.

I did not have a place to stay in Minneapolis following the afternoon practice of the Morningstar Singers, and I was grateful for the kind offer extended by one of the singers. I spent two delightful days with Kristin, her daughter, Ella, and her husband, Jim, her "Handsome Prince." Kristin's life work is community building, and her neighborhood is an excellent example of what that can mean. My timing coincided with a pizza party where neighbors gathered at a brick oven they have built in a vacant lot that also serves as a community garden. Ella was one of five college students in attendance, all home for summer break.

Close to downtown, this area, like all of Minneapolis, is culturally diverse and includes African American and Native American populations, and immigrants from Latin American, Somalia, and Laos. Even within this multi-cultural city, the homogeneous group of singers I met at the Morningstar Singers practice I attended were mostly older white folks like me. It was no different than most of the Threshold Choir chapters I have visited. Having long desired more diversity in Threshold Choir and the other service organizations where I have volunteered, I asked Kristin for her ideas about nurturing inclusion. In response, she told me the story of her Somali immigrant neighbor who, after years of trust-building, has become a treasured friend.

Kristin saw the woman I'll call Amina at the school bus stop every morning, where she kept her head down to avoid eye contact. In time, she learned that Amina had to leave babies at home to walk her school-aged kids to the bus stop. Working a day job and a night job, Amina's husband was not available to help care for their five young children. She did not have a car or the ability to drive.

Eventually, Amina accepted Kristin's offer to walk her school aged children to the bus stop with her own daughter. She was able to assist Amina with other challenges as well, helping her visit the school where her children spent their days, meet their teachers, and attend her first parent-teacher conference.

Kristin had tears in her eyes when she spoke of the hardships Amina faces, and of the friendship that has grown between them. To build alliances, she told me, you must put in the time to build trust.

George Floyd was murdered in this city ten months after my visit. The world-wide outrage ignited by the inhumanity of that violent act confirms that collectively, we recognize the need to change minds and hearts. Kristin's example of building trust by reaching out to offer support when and where it is needed suggests a path to realizing that change.

Finding My Way

At the end of July, I had another close call with a tornado ninety miles north of Minneapolis. As I headed to the Walmart parking lot where I planned to overnight, I started seeing damage from a tornado that had slammed the area. Trees snapped in half damaged roofs, fences, and power lines on both sides of the highway. As dark settled in, I caught sight of an RV lying on its side in a lake. A tornado had ripped through Rice Lake forty-eight hours earlier, and flashing lights on power company trucks signaled electric repairs were still in progress. Kristin's invitation to stay two nights in Minneapolis kept me out of the tornado's path. Thinking about that fortunate timing, a song Lyndsey Scott taught at the *Singing Our Way Back Together* retreat in New York surfaced as a guiding light for this journey, and for life.

The Way Knows the Way
by Lyndsey Scott

You don't have to know the way;
the way knows the way.
You don't have to plan the way,
trust the way, feel your way.
The way knows, the way knows,
the way knows the way.

My windshield was plastered with an ugly mosquito stew by the time I reached northern Minnesota, the home of the Lovely Loon Threshold Choir and my friend, Lulu. An explosion of color blooming in her yard confirmed I had found the right place. Her garden was as vivacious as Lulu, with whom I had spent time at gatherings, and on phone conferences as part of Songleader Flight School. We also share a mutual friend in river raft guide, Valerie, who, decades ago, was Lulu's roommate in Napa Valley. Lulu is more at home in free-spirited California than here in this traditional neighborhood in Coleraine, a town of 1,600 inhabitants, where manicured lawns are expected. Growing a pollinator garden in lieu of a lawn earned her a complaint from the city that summer.

I painted the town with Lulu and her kind husband, John, attending a community hot dog dinner in the park, a brass band performance and pie social on the grass outside the Methodist Church, and a potluck at a friend's lakefront house where the songs around the campfire included "Trees Grow Slow." The host of the gathering was a "ricer, " and he explained the process used to gather the wild rice that grows in the northern lakes. I learned it takes two people to pull the rice grass over the canoe and shake off the grain. Of the 1,200 pounds of rice he and his partner gathered last year, he said that only fifty percent of the harvest remains after processing. Divided among the harvesters, each was left with enough rice for a one-year supply distributed among family members.

I joined the Lovely Loons at one of their practices. They are the only Threshold Choir in the area, with the closest neighbor chapter in Menomonie, a four-hour drive. They rolled out the red carpet for me, and for the regular summer visitor who sings with the Villages Threshold Choir in Florida during the long Wisconsin winters. Quick to appreciate new ideas, Lulu adopted Eleanor's method of releasing songs with the lift of an arm, and other ideas carried from other chapters.

Lulu took me with her to sing to a patient who was close to her time. The woman's eyes remained closed for the twenty minutes we softly sang, hummed, and allowed each song to resonate in sacred silence. We came and went quietly knowing the music we shared will deliver whatever the patient needs in that moment.

With Lulu's gifts of a gas contribution and zucchini muffins warm from the oven, I turned toward the west and unknown territory, once again.

Tornado Protection for Jamestown, ND.

CHAPTER 15

A Disturbing Absence of Trees

After a picnic lunch in the shade of a giant roadside Paul Bunyan, I reluctantly left the shining land of 10,000 lakes to cross the great northern prairies. I would be traveling for weeks without touching base with Threshold singers, and expecting little social interaction on this stretch of my journey, the party at the E4 Winery in the cornfields just outside Fargo, North Dakota, was quite a surprise.

Even though I arrived at closing time, I was enthusiastically welcomed by Harvest Host winery owners, Lisa and Greg, and a friendly crowd of locals who were there as part of a Wine Passport weekend. Greg, who has a PhD in chemistry from Stanford University, likes to experiment with different fruit, and as the vegan viticulturist proudly announced, vegetable wines. Cold country wines can be sweet, but I found some drier offerings sumptuous, and was particularly impressed with Greg's dry rhubarb wine. Asked about my travels, a song was requested. I taught the chorus and refrain of *"The Power of Kindness"* a song by MaMuse, and we had a great time singing together. Greg placed big bowls of what he called "Egyptian street food" on the bar and invited all to enjoy the feast.

After that fun party night, I spent a quiet night at Fort Abraham Lincoln State Park on the banks of the Missouri River. The next day, I stopped at the museum of Western novelist Louis L'Amour, the National Bison Museum, and "the largest buffalo statue in the world." In touristy Jamestown, my tornado alert antenna engaged when the sky suddenly darkened while I was eating lunch at a sandwich shop. The young man working the counter put me at ease, explaining that the only tornado known to touch down in Jamestown landed in front of the buffalo statue, where, he was told by his mother, it was frightened away by that powerful protector of the town. No tornadoes have dared touch down in Jamestown since.

As I continued traveling west, the North Dakota topography transitioned from cornfields and prairie that stretch to the horizon, to rolling hills, buttes, curious cone-shaped hills, and finally, to the dramatic gorges and spires of North Dakota's Badlands. Road trips feed a compelling urge to see what miracle waits around each bend in the road, and the Painted Canyon in the Theodore Roosevelt National Park is one of those miracles. The cleansing scent of sage filled the air as I climbed out of the van to get a better look at the weather-carved stone walls in the maze of colorful canyons hundreds of feet below the park lookout.

Medora, the small town at the south entrance to the National Park, is a reborn historic town in the same way that Monterey's Cannery Row has been reconstructed to attract tourists. In 1964, Harold Schaffer reopened the shuttered hotel, renaming it the "Rough Riders Hotel," and produced the popular Medora Musical.

Every night of the week during tourist season, over 1,000 people flock to the gulch that serves as an outdoor amphitheater to see Medora's old-style variety show. The spotlight is on Teddy Roosevelt's visit to the Dakota Territory to hunt bison in 1883. The high energy program includes a talented young cast singing and dancing to the music of a Western-style band; think *Buffalo Bill Cody's Wild West Show* meets *Oklahoma*. The grand finale included a prayer, a giant American flag projected on the canyon walls, speakers blasting the "Star Spangled Banner," a thundering rush of horse riders, and fireworks.

Camping at a national forest campground on the sage-infused prairielands west of Medora, I enjoyed a spectacular night sky, a hot shower, and a water tank refill, all for $6.00. Following the road to Glacier National Park through the vast grasslands that were once the home of thriving tribal nations and millions of grazing bison made me feel very small indeed.

The Poetry of Trees

Long hours crossing the prairie in oppressive summer heat had me scanning the horizon for shade to cool down Wanda, and my struggling little refrigerator. There was none. Forests graced much of the land I passed through on this trip, and the absence of trees on the northern plains was unsettling.

The sky, the fields, and even the soil are monochrome yellow at this time of year. The sea of chest-high wheat offered little protection from the cruel sun for the isolated houses and barns I passed. With no trees in sight, I have to wonder how these determined inhabitants find wood for fuel, fencing, building their homes, and everything else we depend on from this precious resource. In addition to practical needs, the steadfast farmers and ranchers in this region do not know the comforts trees could provide. It hurts me to think of people living without the poetry of trees: the flowering in the spring, the beauty of seasonal colors, the offerings of fruit and nuts, the climbing possibilities, tire swings hung from accommodating boughs, picnicking in shaded yards, and the marvel of nesting songbirds. The abandoned weather-beaten homesteads that dot the landscape are evidence of the overwhelming challenges faced by those who choose to make the prairie their home.

Lonely Highways.

I was winging it on this stretch of unknown territory, searching for places to overnight at the close of each day. Crossing into Montana, I stumbled upon Ft. Peck, the reservoir that is the largest body of water in the state. I camped on a sand spit with water on three sides and the lights of the four-mile-long dam and power plant sparkling in the distance. A refreshing morning swim started my day.

With another day of driving with no shade in sight, stopping in full sun in the sweltering heat was not an option.

The wind created by movement was the only way to cool the metal van, so I kept driving. My miraculous little refrigerator is engineered to operate on propane, battery power, or plugged into shore power, but in heat like this, even packing it with ice couldn't cool it enough to keep my groceries from spoiling. While driving, I set the cab air conditioner on full blast to kept myself functioning. At the end of an exhausting day of 98° heat, I turned off the highway to follow directions to a BLM campsite with no idea what I would find at the end of the seven-mile dirt road that sliced through golden wheat fields as far as the eye can see. I was tired, it was time to stop driving and prepare my evening meal.

Conscious of black storm clouds in the distance, an eerie stillness in the air, and the deeply rutted dirt road of this deserted campground, I chose a spot on high ground with a spectacular view of the sprawling reservoir shining in the tangerine sunset. Seeking seclusion in nature at free and inexpensive campgrounds and dispersed camping on National Forest and BLM lands meant being without cell service and any contact with the outside world. I felt a combination of elation at being completely alone, and apprehension at having no other campers in sight and no way to call for help. The knowledge that before the onset of smartphones, I had traveled and tent camped alone for fifty years without a need for technology helped put my fears in perspective. Even so, I never did entirely shake the perception that I wasn't safe without cell phone connectivity. When I found myself totally alone in nature, shifting my focus to the beauty of the surroundings restored a feeling of well-being.

Pulling out binoculars, I watched birds foraging for their evening meal. It was just me, a pair of storks, a few graceful terns extracting fish from the glassy calm water, some noisy geese, and an army of hungry mosquitoes. I doused myself with repellent and started a walkabout, but when the repellent, combined with madly waving arms, didn't keep the little beasties away, I retreated to the protection of the van. I had packed a head net for just such an occasion, but as baffling as it was, I couldn't find it in my tiny living space. Losing things was a phenomenon that often occurred in the tightly packed van.

While I chowed down on a Cajun veggie burger and fresh corn on the cob, a glimpse of a young man running along the water's edge alerted me to the fact that another vehicle had arrived and parked near the water. I had neighbors. After dark, Tate and his mother, Dana, paid a visit to tell me their car was stuck in the mud. They asked if I could give them a ride up the road to a place where they could call a tow truck in the morning, insisting it could wait until then.

Of course, I wanted to do whatever I could to help, but talking required an open window, and mosquitoes were pouring in with every word we exchanged. I swatted and fanned as we conversed, but it was of no use; mosquitoes were claiming my shelter for all-night feasting. Unwilling to climb out into the mosquito-frenzied night to chat with them, the situation forced me to cut the conversation short. I promised I wouldn't leave without them in the morning, and they hiked back to their SUV.

I admit that I'm a mosquito wimp. In Minnesota, on the evening I hesitated to make the mosquito-infested crossing through the garden jungle that lay between John and Lulu's house and my van, John had to urge me on with a "Buck up." Maybe you will think better of me knowing that the little California beach town I called home for the past thirteen years is pretty much pest-free, unless you consider migrating Monarch butterflies pests. Window screens are a rare sight in Butterfly Town. I choose to stay indoors as night falls in mosquito country.

Between the mosquitoes and the weather, it would be a long night. The radio that day had warned of a high risk of fires ignited by lightning, and storm clouds were headed our way. I felt compelled to stay awake, on fire patrol, knowing that my mud-mired friends would need Wanda and me for escape should a prairie fire start. For hours, the slow-moving storm pummeled the area with thunder and lightning, with some of those strikes carving a jagged path from the sky to the fields of wheat surrounding the reservoir. Ominously, not a drop of rain fell. I would have fled the area were it not for my commitment to my marooned neighbors. Instead, I prepared Wanda for a quick rescue and kept a nervous watch. I was scared. The night called for prayers, and mine came in the form of spirituals; "All Through the Night," "The Storm is Passing Over," and "Hallelujah." It was after 4:00 a.m. when stars appeared, the signal it was safe to close my eyes.

When morning came, I offered Dana and Tate coffee, blueberries, and yogurt before ferrying them a few miles up the road to a spot where there was cell reception. I wanted to stay until help arrived, but they insisted I continue on my journey, so I embarked on another long day of driving. Summer heat rippled the air, masquerading as water in the dips of the road while isolated mirage towns where grain elevators, silos, and train tracks flashed by with no services for travelers.

I needed a place to park for the night before I could check into my campsite at Glacier. In unfamiliar territory like this, finding somewhere to sleep can be stressful. Along this stretch of lonely highway surrounded by wheat fields, there are no rest stops and no opportunities to pull off the road. Finding an opening at the only RV park on the route to Glacier, I made an online booking despite the absurd price. Two dazed men wandering in the middle of the road near an abandoned coffee stand built in the shape of a teepee slowed traffic entering Browning, the headquarters of the Blackfeet Indian Reservation.

Most of the homes scattered in and around this town suffered peeling paint, missing windows, and roofs with blue tarps anchored by tires, but the distant view of the jagged Lewis Mountain Range rising dramatically from the flat prairie is majestic. I will be forever haunted by the sight of a desperate black horse with no escape from the punishing heat, leaning into the side of a building to take advantage of the little bit of shade created by the overhang of the roof eave.

A stop at Teeples IGA, the only market in town, exposed a food desert with jacked-up prices and a lack of selection, unless you are shopping for Kool-Aid, which is available in a vast selection of flavors and packaging. Despite the meager offerings, the market provides a gathering place for the town of 1,000 inhabitants where all are known by name and the native language is spoken. Located at the end of a dirt road, past acres of horse stables, Running Wolf Campground offered a spectacular view of the sun setting behind the mountaintops in the distance, a clean bathroom, and a warm shower.

Where Grizzlies Roam

Continuing on to Glacier National Park in the morning, I crossed the forty-seven miles of humble plains that is reservation land to reach the winding road that leads up the mountainside to the park entrance. There is a rawness to this land where wind, rain, and freezing temperatures continually reshape the glacier-carved stones. The park glows with "Yosemite" grandeur and pristine glacial lakes reflect the magnificence of the scenery. The opportunity to witness the power of the elements draws us to landscapes like this. I arrived during the peak of the summer season when the park is mobbed with happy hikers, mountain bikers, and families, here to marvel at the surroundings. The fact that few glaciers remain in the park surely adds to the desire to see these remnants of the past while it is still possible.

At the Visitor Center, I learned about the park, the animals that inhabit the area, and the Native people who lost their land to the park in the treaty signed in 1896. The Blackfeet Nation lost their ceremonial lands, herbs and medicinal plants, and the lakes, rivers, and big game that do not exist on the grasslands around the park where the reservation was established. The progression of snaggle-toothed ridges standing sentry over the park that we call the Continental Divide is the "Backbone of the World" to the indigenous people of this region.

A free hikers' shuttle travels the winding Going-to-the-Sun-Road that crosses the park, and I spent the rest of the day "joy-riding" to get the lay of the land. From the shuttle, glimpses of three of the twenty-four remaining glaciers can be seen. All are facing declassification due to melting. The shuttle also offers an excellent way to view wildlife. I missed the mama grizzly with three cubs that riders saw standing next to the road that morning, but I did get a close-up view of bighorn sheep grazing near one of the shuttle stops.

After a couple of nights at St. Mary's campground, the desire to move to a more rustic setting in the park motivated me to wait in line for a space at the Rising Sun Campground on my third day in the park. Setting my alarm for the first time in months, I arrived at 6:50 a.m. to be eighth in line at the campground entry. The woman in the fifth spot told me she had arrived at 5:30. The line of cars grew to more than twenty as we waited for the ranger carrying a clipboard to tell us what came next. At 7:30, we were gathered in a circle for an orientation. I had a spot!

The ranger read the campground rules and told us this is the campground most frequented by wild animals. With so many grizzlies and black bears around, stiff fines and confiscations are in store for any camper who leaves food, cooking utensils, or anything else with a tempting scent unattended outside their vehicle. The phrase, "A fed bear is a dead bear," is regularly used by park staff to explain how serious this is.

The ranger went on to say that when she reached this

part of her talk the morning before, an enormous male grizzly passed twenty feet behind her, as if on cue, and continued his amble through the campground unfazed by the crowd. She told us about the relocation of three black bears hanging around the campground a week earlier that had opened the territory for new bears to move in. There was concern that this grizzly may have taken advantage of the opening.

My campsite was nestled against a mountainside. It offered huckleberries, privacy, and a view of magenta fireweed blooming on slopes burned in the 2015 fire that was stopped when it reached the defensible space of the campground. I had scored three nights in campground nirvana with a clear stream, trails to St. Mary's Lake, a shuttle stop, and a General Store within walking distance.

I met Tom (the English version of the longer native language name the other shuttle drivers called him) on the day he was in charge of crowd control at the Visitor Center shuttle stop where I was waiting for a ride back to my campsite. Because it took nearly an hour for the shuttle to appear, we had a good talk.

When I commented that shuttle drivers must enjoy being the heroes who rescue grateful hikers at the end of the trail, he told me that not all riders are grateful. Tom explained that just the day before, a passenger entering his bus made an offensive comment when he saw the driver was a Native man. Tom wasn't having it on his watch. He confronted the man, telling him to get off the bus, and radioed the other drivers not to pick him up. After the affronting passenger was forced to wait at the bus stop for hours, Tom finally stopped for him.

Before letting the guy onto the bus, Tom asked if he understood why he was asked to get off, and no other drivers would stop for him. The man said that he did, and he apologized for the comment he made. The story made me proud of Tom, and mindful of the need to take a stand against hateful language.

Hearing that a grizzly was in the meadow near the campground just as I was preparing to leave the park, I jumped on the opportunity. Walking to a place where I could see the bear foraging about 300 yards from the road, I was feeling a bit exposed when a family watching from the bed of their pickup truck invited me to climb in. With binoculars, I had an excellent view of the gigantic hump-backed bear with powerful haunches and bleached fur on his face and chest. I watched as he retreated into denser vegetation. Check, grizzly bear seen.

Finding it difficult to leave these spectacular mountains, I decided to continue north to the Waterton Lakes National Park, a continuation of the magnificent park on the Canadian side of the border. The scenic drive wound past sacred Chief Mountain and across the Canadian boundary to the entrance to the park. The $10.00 entry fee was a pleasant surprise considering the daily entry fee at neighboring Glacier National Park is $35.00. I am grateful that my Lifetime Golden Age Park Pass provides free admission and reduced camping costs at National Parks in the US, and I thank my friend, Keith, who encouraged me to buy the pass when I became eligible at sixty-two. At that time, the pass cost only $10.00, but even at the current cost of $80.00, a life-time National Parks Pass is worth the cost.

Just inside the Waterton Lakes National Park gate, the devastation of a 2017 fire that burned 50,000 acres of forests in the park was on full display. The fire was so hot that it destroyed major roads still closed two years later. Passing through twelve miles of charred stumps where forest once stood, I came to the shining lake and lovely swimming beaches that surround the charming (and very expensive) town of Waterton. A swim in one of the many lakes in the park was the highlight of my evening. I spent two nights camping at a lackluster campground five miles from the park, and prepared and ate my meals and swam at a picnic area just outside the park entry, where I had an entire lake to myself. The prospect of sharing my lakeside haven with bears kept me close to the van.

The Oldest Person in Fernie

With weeks before my next scheduled stop in Sandpoint, Idaho, I followed Crow's Nest Highway through Canada's Livingston Mountains and a succession small coal mining towns before landing in Fernie. Downtown Fernie stopped me in my tracks with its awe-inspiring view of the "Three Sisters" mountains, rushing river, and large wooded parks. Either the residents of this charming little town are all of child-bearing age, or there is something in the water; I don't think I have ever seen so many beautiful, athletic young families. Just as traffic stopped for the mother geese I saw herding their spring goslings across busy streets in New England, cars in Fernie stop for tattooed, mountain bike-riding mamas herding helmeted little ones on their own mountain bikes. With bicycles the main mode of transportation in summer, the sidewalks buzzed with the activity of helmet-carrying locals ducking in and out of vegetarian restaurants, brew pubs, sidewalk cafés, art galleries, and sporting goods stores. A funky vibe made me feel at home here, even though I didn't exactly blend.

There was plenty to do in Fernie. I drove to the ski resort where I saw bikes carried up the mountain in the bucket seats of the ski lift. At an afternoon painting class I attended at the downtown art center, the "watercolors" we used were tinctures prepared by an environmentally focused instructor using plants that are invasive species in the area. How hip is that? I soon had the art class singing a call and response song with words by Leonard Cohen, "Forget your Perfect Offering." I also attended the Wapiti Music Festival and danced to the music of bands with names like Fake Shark and Mountain Sound. The festival offered the $45.00 daily entry fee to seniors for $5.00. I can only imagine that was possible because there were so few of us in this town.

Parked alongside the Elk River just south of town, I could leave curtains open to the exquisite scenery and blue skies. I took great pleasure being awakened each night by moonlight licking my face.

I left Fernie excited about celebrating my birthday with a cherished tradition; staying up all night to watch the Perseids meteor shower. Recurring phenomena like meteor showers are reminders of the cycles of which we are all a part. I consider it an act of devotion to honor our great earth mother by putting aside lesser demands, like sleep, to observe and appreciate her extraordinary gifts. Whether the event is a meteor shower, eclipse, solstice, sunset, or even the falling rain, I'm all in.

Sky Watching.

This year, the meteor shower was not visible due to cloud cover, so I settled for going to the movies to see *The Lion King*, eating uninspired chocolate birthday cake from Walmart, and overnighting in the brightly lit Walmart parking lot in Cranbrook, B.C., with a dozen other RVers.

Wanda is well equipped for dry camping (no electrical, water, or sewer hookups), but parking lots are my last choice for nighttime parking. Campers seeking privacy in those very public places cover windows to block the bright lights and the outside world. Not having a view of the night sky is a high price to pay for free parking.

Two-thirds of the residents in the US cannot see the Milky Way due to light pollution. I often think about how different nights must have been before electricity, when the sky inspired mankind with myth and magic, and reading the stars was how we navigated the planet. Speaking for myself, much of the lure of camping is being outdoors under the night sky.

CHAPTER 16

Good Vibrations

After crossing back into the US, I reached the sparkling gem that is Sandpoint, Idaho. Built on pristine Lake Pend Oreille, the 111 miles of coastline at the convergence of three mountain ranges is a paradise for outdoor enthusiasts who appreciate snow and long winters. Perky chose this idyllic location as her home forty years ago, and since my last visit, a Threshold Choir has been established in town. Even though I divorced her brother in 1973, Perky has always made me feel part of the family. We hiked to a waterfall, played at the lake with her sweet grandkids, shared a lakeside dinner with her grown sons and the whole family, and ate huckleberries from the tremendous stash that she foraged to fill her freezer.

Practicing with the Sandpoint Threshold Singers was a wonderful experience. This vibrant group enjoys regular social activities together. A three-day retreat each year and trainings, such as the anchor training scheduled for the coming week, support the strong bond among choir members. To grow the choir, the director requested that each choir member recruit someone new and take on the role of buddy/mentor for the new member.

Invited to lunch at the home of the Sandpoint choir director, I asked Marilyn and her musician husband, Dave, their thoughts on how singing and making music together bond us. Dave told of the connection he feels from the vibrational aspect of making music together. He spoke of how the unique vibrations musicians create are felt in the body, not the brain. I have felt that sensation when choir members match a pitch so precisely it creates a vibration that rings like a bell. Dave's statement, "Music is a way to communicate energy," helps explain how songs have the power to penetrate the surface and touch a place deep within.

In large choirs, where we sing in parts, I am aware that I feel most aligned with singers who are close to me in the soprano section. In those groups, hearing other parts can be difficult, if not impossible, and it falls on the director to balance the various parts of the music, not the singers. Crammed in tightly with the other singers in the sections of a choral group, finding and singing the same pitches is easier. When we get it right, we ride the same wavelength and feel the same vibrations, with breathing and heartbeats synchronized.

Scientific studies measuring the pulse of choir singers confirm that oxygen and blood course through the bodies of those singers in rhythmic unison,[45] but they cannot tell us what effect that may have on a group of people. It is hard to imagine that the coordinated breathing and heartbeats we experience as we sing together would not have a unifying effect. One song, one breath, one heart.

Grateful for the visit with family and a chance to sing with the Sandpoint chapter, I was also pleased to dodge the bullet of running into my second "wasband," who purchased a home in Sandpoint a number of years ago. Jim and I found Maui too small for the two of us after our divorce in 1986. Sandpoint is even smaller. I ask you, what are the odds that my long-divorced second husband from Maui would settle in the same remote town that is the home of the sister of my first husband?

Montana's Buried Treasure

The drive from northern Idaho to Missoula, Montana, follows the Lewis and Clark Rivers. Winding through picturesque gorges, the road is flanked by menacing rock slides that pour down the faces of the steep slopes. In Glacier Park, I learned that cycles of freezing and thawing are not the only forces at work to send rocks tumbling downhill. The action of grizzlies in their search for tasty moths and grubs, the scrambling of big horn sheep and mountain goats, and even the digging of little ground squirrels, also trigger slides. One can't help but be awed by the grandeur of this unsettled landscape.

In the tiny town of Thompson Falls, set against a backdrop of enormous rock slides, I made lunch and ate at a shaded picnic table next to the Lewis River. To my surprise, two different drivers slowed their cars to wave and smile at me. At first, I wondered if it was a case of mistaken identity, but with my camper van visibly parked next to the table, these passers by had to know I was a transient, a wanderer, a drifter. In small towns where families have lived for generations, I always feel like a rootless outsider. The fact that the locals were so friendly caught me off guard. It may be that the wandering lifestyle appeals to those individuals and the greeting was their way of letting me know that they know wanderlust, either by experience or by desire. Perhaps, the fact I am living the dream is an inspiration to them. More likely, I'm overthinking this, and they are just a friendly lot here in rural Montana.

Many of the sleepy towns I passed through were bawdy boom towns until the gold or silver ran out, but Helena is not a boom-and-bust town. The capital of Montana has the bragging right to have once claimed more millionaires per capita than any other US city, a legacy visible in the grand civic buildings and mansions built when gold was discovered here in 1864. The mine at the Last Chance Gulch yielded $19 million in gold over a four-year period.

I was in town to meet up with a high school friend I hadn't seen in decades. Thanks to Facebook, we were able to reconnect. I parked in the driveway of Charlie and Lynn's hillside home, and Charlie gave me a guided tour. We walked historic downtown Helena and visited a local sculptor before stopping for a beer in a popular brewery where one of Charlie's photos of Glacier National Park covers an entire wall.

The next stop, Butte, Montana, is not so grand. A Threshold Choir visit called me to this active mining town in the shadow of the Continental Divide, where a mammoth copper and zinc mine dominates the landscape and the economy of the city. Entering Butte, I was fixated on the scar that was once a mountain, with its city-sized pit where the earth's skin has been peeled away to expose raw soil streaked red, orange, and yellow with precious minerals. The crater is now actively blasted, and chiseled by bulldozers and other heavy mining equipment, a process that has replaced the dangerous, soul-numbing work of tunneling underground. This is the second gigantic pit in town; the first was closed and filled with water to become a toxic lake and Superfund cleanup site.

Newer methods employed to extract minerals from the mountain are touted as cleaner, but heavy metals in the air and water are issues of concern for the townspeople.

I was curious about the white substance that looked like spilled milk washing down the streets when it rained. The mines in this town provided forty-one percent of the nation's copper when it was needed to wire the country for electricity, and successful mine owners from Butte's heyday built their mansions in nearby Helena.

The director of the Butte Montana Threshold Singers graciously arranged a get-together for my visit, even though the choir had taken the month of August off. Ana is no shrinking violet with her bright red hair and stylish asymmetrical hairdo. She is a hospice volunteer coordinator, trainer, and chaplain, a mother of four adopted trans-racial kids (she explained this means the parents and kids are of different races), and the founder and director of the Butte Montana Threshold Singers. After a long work-day, she hosted the choir at her home and prepared dinner for us. We sang together, talked about bedside singing, and I shared songs and stories from my trip.

After two days and nights in Butte I was won over by its hardworking citizens and charmed by the modest "company housing" Victorians from a bygone era. I felt I had stepped back in time to a working-class town where all residents share the same values. Ana is proud of the town's union history, calling Butte a blue blip in an otherwise red state. Besides drawing immigrants from around the world to work in the mines, Butte is famous for being the "Gibraltar of Unionism" because of the relentless battles to successfully organize miners between the 1890s and 1930s.

Moving east along Highway 90, I was struck by the contrast between Butte and my next stop, Bozeman, Montana, where modern architecture and a gentrified downtown shine with stylish restaurants and breweries. I was an awestruck kid again seeing the fossils, skulls, skeleton collection, and the enormous tyrannosaurus rex at the University of Montana Museum of the Rockies. Gold, silver, and copper aren't the only treasures buried in this state.

Arriving in Bozeman on a weekend limited my overnight options to a Walmart parking lot. The uncomfortable setting was a messy mix of expensive new RVs and enormous fifth-wheel trailers taking up multiple spaces, converted school buses, and people sleeping in cars with trash and cigarette butts littering the pavement. An early morning departure would have me enjoying the peace of the forest again.

A Sacred Land

With two nights before my campsite in Yellowstone National Park would be available, a Forest Service campground on the Madison River provided a front row seat for watching fly fishers performing their graceful ballet with slender line, air, and water.

Inside Yellowstone, the road follows the Madison River through pine forests and tremendous mountains of crumbling stone, but a change had occurred. This is sacred land, protected and honored for what it is. No homes, ranches, or shopping centers alter the landscape. Within moments of entering this Shangri La, elk stopping traffic within sight of a moose grassing in the river were signs that I had entered a wild kingdom. Plumes of steam rising high in the intensely blue sky drew me to my next stop, the Lower Geyser Basin, where a single bison stood in sight of the parking lot as if it was a prop, a tame "Greeting Bison" representing the majesty of the park.

Greeted by a Yellowstone Icon.

Visitors are required to maintain a distance of twenty-five yards from wildlife, 100 yards from bears and wolves, but I was wary being that close to bison. There is no telling what the powerful beasts with their deceptively peaceful demeanor might be thinking, and there have been plenty of bison gorings to bear this out. The earth, too, has a certain dangerous beauty in Yellowstone. The smell of sulfur leaves little doubt that the luminous boiling pools, bubbling mud pots, and fitful geysers offer a tip of the iceberg view of what lies below. The mercurial ground is raw and alive here.

Signs warn visitors to stay on the boardwalks with pictographs showing what looks like solid ground but is actually a thin crust that can break through, dropping those who dare to step off the boardwalk into the boiling threat below. Intrigued by the bison hoof tracks and dung visible on the ground around the geysers and pools, I asked a ranger about this. I was told that bison intuitively know where to step, but on occasion, one will break through the surface to be swallowed by an unforgiving bubbling cauldron where the carcass is cooked until it is completely decomposed.

Yellowstone is a live volcano caldera. With its clever system of geysers to release pressure, the surface is continually in flux and subject to the whims of earthquake swarms and the explosive thermal force that festers just below the surface. After living with volcanoes in Hawaii, and with dynamic faults and earthquakes in California, I have fear and respect for the unpredictable forces deep within the earth.

In 1872, a time when this nation was encouraging settlement, the United States Congress courageously established Yellowstone National Park, our first National Park, preserving this unique landscape for the public. With all that has changed over the past 150 years, the ability to witness free-ranging bison, elk, and bears in their natural habitat would not be available to most of us without that action. Our National Parks make me proud.

A young German couple camping next to me in a rented RV joined me at my campfire one night. They told me that there are no National Parks in their country. The slogan, "Yellowstone Forever," is an important reminder that insuring the perpetuity of the park requires vigilance to prevent political interests and greed from compromising our hard-won public lands.

A Change in Course

On my last morning in Yellowstone National Park, anxious to write about an encounter with rutting bison the previous day, I opened my laptop to find the screen damaged. On this fateful morning, my compulsion to write had me typing around a prism of color that had exploded in the center of the laptop screen until horizontal and vertical lines expanding from the damaged center made the typing vanish. For years, I have done all of my writing on computer. The ability to save, edit, and systematically file my work on a computer replaced the scraps of paper and countless notebooks where I once recorded my reflections. Not having access to my computer felt like having my hands tied behind my back.

I panicked. I risked losing excel spreadsheets with my records of the journey, contacts, and interviews with choir members. It had been some time since I backed-up my computer to the external drive I carried, and without regular internet connection, I was not plugged into cloud back-up.

My next scheduled stop was the Grand Canyon, where I had reserved a campsite in the National Park for a week. The plan to head south from Yellowstone, through the Grand Tetons, Wyoming, and Utah promised to be an exciting adventure. Only Salt Lake City offered an Apple repair option and a Threshold Choir, but that didn't have much appeal. The memory of the unfriendly welcome

I received there in 1973 while traveling in a van with a Navajo turquoise trader who wore buckskin pants, no shirt, and feathers tied in his long unruly hair, made me less than enthusiastic about returning to the area. A shimmy in the brakes also had me concerned about that mountainous route.

Even before this calamity, I had considered rerouting my trip to the Pacific Northwest. At this point in the journey, I was feeling overwhelmed by the wonder of all that I was experiencing. I longed for the reassurance of familiarity, the ocean, cool nights in the forests, and my people.

Whenever I became exhausted swimming in a sea of solitude, I reached for the lifeline of connection. The realization that part of my work on this journey is to be aware of my needs, and to do what feeds my joy, was slow in coming. I was in new territory at this particular juncture. The rare and enviable ability to change course on a whim had arrived. It took a broken computer and wonky brakes to motivate me to assess my needs and make adjustments accordingly.

I canceled my Grand Canyon reservation and set my course for Boise, Idaho, where there is an Apple store, a step-granddaughter with a fourteen-month-old baby, a Threshold Choir, a community singing circle, and plenty of options for brake repairs.

The Kindness of Strangers

It took three days to get to Boise. The heat was intense as I drove through otherworldly landscapes and twisted black lava fields where a lack of topsoil exposed volcanic bedrock on this stretch of the plains. A two-day visit with Holly, the grown-up version of the little girl who spent Christmas holidays with me baking cookies and making gingerbread houses, recharged my battery. Her happy baby girl, Stella, entertained us while we caught up on the gap years.

In Boise, I surrendered my computer at the Apple store. I was told my work would be saved and the laptop repair would take five days. This was good news, but being without my computer for another five days would be a challenge. Van repairs would also mean that my bedroom would be unavailable for a few days.

Just outside of Boise, Idaho, the director of the Nampa Threshold Singers, extended enormous kindness. Marsha offered her air-conditioned guest room for as long as I needed it. She fed me and drove me back and forth for days of repairs at two different shops. I was able to participate in a Nampa chapter practice, and spent five days with Marcia and her happy baby girl, a ten-month-old golden retriever, also named Stella.

Marcia Bernstein was a member of the Placerville Threshold Singers in California before moving to Nampa. When I asked what singing at bedsides means to her, she answered as other choir members have, that it provides a way to be of service. Marcia explained that she started the choir in Nampa because of a pressing need to "step outside of myself." In addition to the service aspect, she said she appreciates the family that forms within chapters. After moving to Nampa, she missed the closeness she had with choir members in Placerville, a bond she now enjoys with members of the Nampa Threshold Singers.

When I thanked Marcia for all she had done for me, she made it clear that she considers it natural to help where help is needed. Depending on the "kindness of strangers" like Blanche DuBois, in *A Streetcar Named Desire*, is both humbling and reassuring.

Before leaving the area, I went to hear jazz at the Old Boise State Penitentiary, now a botanical garden and music venue, with a songleader friend from Songleader Flight School who lives in Boise. Jolene and I first met as participants in Lisa's singing and yoga retreat in Bali in 2016. When a thunderstorm suddenly rolled in, powerful wind gusts, lightning, thunder, and rain stopped the show, but it did not stop us from touring the gardens in the wild wind and rain.

With my computer and van repaired, I followed a section of the Oregon Trail toward the Pacific Northwest. It was close to 100° degrees when I stopped at the shady rest stop at Dead Man Pass and read about the dangers pioneers faced crossing these mountains. A geologist once told me that our highways follow the footpaths the first humans followed, and the trails our ancestors chose to follow were created by the migrations of animals, starting with the movement of prehistoric animals. This mountain pass was likely established by the lumbering of mammoths long before 400,000 settlers in covered wagons made the crossing.

Favorable Winds

I was on my way to Washington when the sad news reached me. On September 2, 2019, a dive boat accident took the lives of thirty-four people near the Channel Islands off the coast of Santa Barbara. The incident generated shock and grief. Fourteen of the passengers lost on the *Conception* were from Santa Cruz, and my friend, Susan, lost her forty-year-old daughter in the tragedy.

When a charter sailboat company in Santa Cruz invited family members to participate in a memorial sail, eighteen Santa Cruz Threshold Singers gathered on the dock to sing for those grieving passengers. Marti Mariette, the director of the choir, explained that choir members "felt compelled to continue singing until the boat was out of sight."

Susan Moren was one of the passengers on that memorial sail. She told me that hearing the singing on the dock while boarding the sailboat "made me feel held, blessed." She shared how the songs transformed the boat to sacred space, setting the tone for the sail. "We were fourteen families, unknown to each other. The singing brought us together by creating a comfort zone, helping people focus on their hearts." Susan said that hearing the singing continue as the boat sailed away from the dock was a send-off that "felt like favorable winds."

A cool night in misty clouds at the foot of Mt. Rainier marked my return to Washington. I slept at a rest stop next to a station wagon packed with camouflage garbed deer hunters partying until they drove away at the break of dawn.

Under the Spell of the Hoh Rainforest.

Chapter 17

Tako Eye Transformation

The first stop on the Olympic Peninsula was "Sunny Sequim," where Nancy, a member of the choir in Port Angeles, offered her driveway and hospitality. The towering Olympic Mountains south of Sequim form a barrier to rain, favoring this location with a dryer climate than any other spot on the rainy peninsula. In Hawaiian, a blessed location such as this is a *pukalani*, a hole in the heavens where the sun peeks through.

The Clallam County Threshold Choir practice I attended in Port Angeles started with meditation followed by vocal warm-ups. The five anchors who lead singing at bedsides took turns leading the circle. A discussion concerning a recent challenge that had occurred at a bedside followed. Astrid, who founded this chapter, was my roommate in 2017 at the dorms where we stayed for the All Choir Gathering in Portland.

With the opportunity to revisit a friend made a year earlier, I rode the walk-on ferry across the Salish Sea to Victoria, stayed in Susannah's guest room for a night, and returned to Port Angeles the next evening. She was waiting at the dock when I arrived. We walked around the majestic city for a bit before heading to her sweet home. We laughed, sang, ate fresh salmon, and went to the farmer's market where I was introduced to Empress Gin and locally crafted tonics. This well-traveled retired librarian told me that entertaining guests from far and wide has replaced her passion for travel. My gracious host's kind spirit and playfulness made for a perfect visit. I'm so grateful for the warm welcome.

Returning to Washington, I camped at Port Townsend State Park. Mornings come slowly in the tall trees. Parked in the shadows of a forest so dense that no sun penetrates, I gave myself permission to spend those soft mornings drifting in and out of dream time. One of the best things about post-retirement life has been living without the dictates of an alarm clock. Gazing out at the trees from the comfort of my bed is the perfect way to ease into a day.

On one of those mornings when I was feeling particularly sleepy, I was pushing to get out of bed when I heard myself singing, "When the Red, Red Robin Comes Bob, Bob, Bobbin' Along." The words flowed out of my mouth unimpeded by thought. The dated song choice only made sense when I got to the verse, "Wake up, wake up you sleepy head, get up, get up, get out of bed, cheer up, cheer up the sun is red, live, love, laugh, and be happy."

Exploring the area, I headed to the Olympic National Park and the wet and wild west coast of the Olympic Peninsula. Within the park, I snagged a night in the campground at Sol Duc Springs Resort and spent an afternoon soaking in the mineral hot springs there. At Neah Bay, I ate fry bread and visited the Makah Cultural and Research Center to learn about the history and art of the Native tribes of the peninsula. At Mora Campground, the old growth forest exerts a powerful presence. Washington's Olympic Peninsula is home to the largest western red cedar, Sitka spruce, and Douglas fir in the world, and the largest yellow cedar, western hemlock, mountain hemlock, and Engelmann spruce in the country.

Trees love the moisture-rich climate of the western shores of Washington's Olympic Peninsula, and the timber industry was the main source of livelihood for the people living here until the mid-1970s, when the spotted owl and a bitter battle between environmentalists and the timber industry led to limitations on clear-cutting. The change in timber harvesting has allowed forests to reclaim the land, and silted rivers that have been restored now provide important habitat needed for salmon, and other compromised wildlife in the region, to make a comeback. The thriving forests are a draw for tourists. With 3.25 million people visiting Washington's Olympic National Park in 2019, tourism jobs are bringing towns like Forks back to life after they had been financially devastated when the timber industry failed. The highway to Hoh Rain Forest weaves through these happy forests, and through Forks, home of the *Twilight* vampire series.

The Enchantment

Upper Hoh Road doesn't climb up into the mountains as I was expecting; it follows the Hoh River into a deep ravine, a journey that felt like tunneling into Middle Earth. Inside this primeval rain forest, dense, moisture-laden air creates a greenhouse where vegetation and all manner of life thrive. The Hoh campground was quiet and inviting with the busy summer season over. As the sun was setting, haunting cries of rutting elk echoed in the trees as I left camp to follow a narrow trail winding through chest-high ferns and pools of crystal water. My timing couldn't have been any better; by the end of the week Forest Service campgrounds, and some State and

National Park campgrounds, including this one, would close for the season.

On a morning hike in Hoh's emerald forest, I entered an enchanted world teeming with layers of life that glow with psychedelic intensity. A thriving interdependent system is clearly visible here: lichen hanging from limbs above, mosses carpeting all living and non-living matter on the forest floor, and ferns and shrubs rooted in the mosses. Impressive shiny-backed beetles crisscrossed the path, ignoring me as they scurried along fulfilling their role in this ecosystem. There is no separation of life and death here; all are intertwined in the great cycle that is the living, breathing rain forest.

This paradigm of a community thriving on shared resources gave me a visual for the exciting scientific discoveries about the interconnectedness of trees, and entire forests, that I have been reading about in books like *The Hidden Life of Trees*[46] and *Finding the Mother Tree*.[47] A rainforest is a holy place, and witnessing the diversity of life that exists there was transformative.

Turning back toward Port Townsend and civilization, I stopped for another night at Mora campground. Either mushrooms shot up during the week I spent exploring Olympic National Park, or the rain forest awakened my senses to what had gone unseen before. Shifting my gaze from the dizzying tree-tops and misting sky to the earth beneath my feet, a whole world began to come into focus. In this fecund laboratory of fertility, I could see fungi fruiting in endless variety, pushing delicate heads up through the duff, the tree roots, and the cracks in the paved road. I was called to witness the shape-shifting miracle of fungi in their infinite variety of colors and shapes.

I had developed *tako eye,* an expression I heard a Hawaiian chef use to explain the ability to find delicacies hiding in the wild. He told of seeing nothing when he walked Hawaiian reefs looking for tako (the Japanese word for octopus), and how old Japanese fishermen with *tako eye* astounded him with their ability to see the well-camouflaged cephalopods, easily filling their buckets. *Tako eye* for fungi is a gift indeed.

Without enough knowledge to know which mushrooms are safe to eat, and with no books or internet access to identify the toxic from the edible varieties, I was free to appreciate the astounding diversity of design with no concern for discerning which ones could be harvested and eaten. I saw them everywhere.

As the wonders of the forest came into focus, this stay at Mora launched a practice that would be part of my travels going forward. I spent the day gathering cast-off treasures (sticks, leaves, seed droppings, and rocks) to assemble and arrange in a mandala offering to the forest. Andy Goldsworthy's work,[48] and the enchanting offerings of fresh flowers in little palm leaf baskets left in doorways in Bali each morning were my inspiration. I found it satisfying to leave the forest offerings at the campsites where I stayed, it gave me a way to honor those special places with art unique to each site.

My designs were destined to be transformed by wind and rain. Perhaps it is that ephemerality that gives them value. Being reminded that, "You don't own this," helps ground me in gratitude for the gifts that come my way.

Offerings.

The great David La Chapelle told me he didn't record the brilliant tales spun in his intuitive story circles because once spoken, releasing them made room for more to come through. Creativity is a hungry master.

Dams or Salmon

I took a ferry from Port Townsend to Whidbey Island to sing with the chapter there, and to reconnect with friends made last year. At the north end of Whidbey, my spectacular campsite at Deception Pass State Park looked down on Cranberry Lake and Puget Sound. Following a beach trail into the dense forests on the rocky shoreline, I was rewarded with a breathtaking view of the narrow deep water channel that separates Whidbey and Hidalgo Islands, the rickety looking trellis bridge that connects the islands, and sailboats moored in the Caribbean-blue water far below.

On Whidbey, Ellen, a new member of the choir, offered her driveway and we discovered we had much in common. She was ecstatic about her recent move to this lovely island home after two years in an RV. Her experience was not the joyful journey of discovery that I was living. Traveling the country connecting with Threshold Choir chapters has provided purpose and community that most full-time RVers will not find on the road. I was blessed, my journey was "not a caravan of despair," in the words of Rumi.

This time around, the Whidbey Bedside Singers' practice had moved to the common room of a cohousing community, home to a choir member who was receiving hospice care. The sun was shining when I left the scenic jewel that is Whidbey Island to ferry to Washington's mainland. My first stop would be Shoreline, just north of Seattle, where I would park in Robin's driveway, enjoy a hot shower, eat tasty faux crab cakes made with zucchini harvested from her bountiful garden, and dive into a discussion about choir leadership with one of the TCI organization's most devoted leaders.

Seattle is fertile Threshold Choir territory, and at the time of my visit, Robin was leading fifty-three choir members in three separate weekly practices. She also schedules all of the bedside singing. She asks members to pick one of the weekly practices to attend, because, in her opinion, more than twenty members at a practice does not allow sufficient time for each member to check in, something she considers vital for the cohesiveness of the group. Robin's enthusiasm and competence produce a constant stream of requests to join the choir, a logistics problem our little chapter in Pacific Grove would like to have.

Following the Wednesday night choir practice in Seattle, I drove east to Kirkland to join the Evergreen Threshold Singers. After van repairs had forced me to cancel the visit planned a year earlier, I finally had a chance to meet with this illustrious chapter. After singing together for an hour, a group left the practice room to sing at bedsides in the facility. The bedside group consists of different singers each time, giving everyone an opportunity to sing together in a small ensemble. Within the remaining group, Patty, who was directing, demonstrated one of the techniques that Melanie DeMore teaches; repositioning singers within a group to improve the sound balance. The blend of the five singers was clearly improved by the adjustments Patty made to where they stood in relation to each other when singing.

Called to the Sea

With over a week before a return to my son's farm in Oregon, I had time to travel slowly. After another visit with Adina, and an art tour that included Tacoma's Chihuly glass adorned walking bridge, I gave in to the urge to head to an isolated stretch of Washington's southwestern shoreline I hadn't seen. It took hours to reach the isolated little fishing village of Westport, but it was well worth the drive.

A yearning deep within calls me to the water. During the twelve years I lived on Maui, I swam in the friendly sea every day, feeling supported and nurtured by the warm salt water. More of an ocean watcher than swimmer in the chilly sea off the West Coast, I am mesmerized by the glints of light that dance on the surface and the motion of the waves. Whether a churning sea, calm lake, or rushing river, I feel a magnetic draw to water, the mother of all life.

Love of the water is a common thread in my family. My siblings and I grew up competing on swim teams and working out in the lap pool in our backyard. My brother became a Navy SEAL, one sister is a lifeguard, and my other sister became a marine biologist. My sons also love the water; Joe kite surfs and loves to start his days jumping into an icy cold stream, and Kel, who was born on Maui and was swimming before he could walk, bodysurfs at Santa Cruz and Marin County beaches.

Not a Dismal Ditch to Me

Returning to the turbulent mouth of the great Columbia River, the untamed beauty of Washington's beaches and the history of the area called me to Cape Disappointment State Park. On a cliff overlooking the beach, North Head Lighthouse warns navigators of the treacherous waters where the full force of the river and the Pacific collide. Camping next to the park's black sand beach, I spent two full days gathering cast-off shells, crab's claws, and barnacles to create a beach mandala.

I also spent nights at nearby Dismal Ditch Rest Stop, where free riverfront parking offers a spectacular view of the bridge that arcs across the four-and-a-half mile river mouth to Astoria, and the lights of that charming city. Signs at the rest stop explain that this spot on the riverbank was named by Lewis and Clark when they camped here in 1805. Unable to paddle their canoes the last few miles to the sea because of a raging storm, the expedition journal reported the party was forced to stop here, where they were as wet, cold, and hungry as they had been on their entire 8,000-mile journey. After being stranded for eight days, they completed their mission, crossed the channel, and spent the winter on the more hospitable Oregon side of the river.

Navigating the mouth of the Columbia is no less challenging for maritime traffic today. Considered one of the most dangerous ports in the world, it has earned the nickname, "Graveyard of the Pacific." Shifting bars of sediment, and treacherous weather conditions have been the cause of more than 200 shipwrecks at the river mouth since 1792. Coast Guard rescues are regular occurrences here, and the seething water is utilized for training in all weather conditions. I kayaked in the river on an earlier trip, cautiously putting-in several miles inland and sticking close to the shoreline to avoid being sucked into the powerful current.

Despite the dangerous conditions, barges, tugboats, and cargo ships routinely travel the Columbia. A local radio station gives a morning shipping report announcing what ships will be passing through the port that day with their country of origin, the cargo they are carrying, and the time they can be seen passing.

I arrived in Lincoln City on a rare afternoon when Joe and Gretchen's farm was bathed in warm sunlight. On the banks of Schooner Creek, in a forested river gorge between steep mountains, the farm gets over 100 inches of rain a year and very limited sunlight. They have an extensive garden but the growing season is short. The honeybees they housed in boxes Joe built with hand-hewn western hemlock could not survive on their farm, despite the supplemental feeding they did.

During my visit, cucumbers and apples were bountiful, and we foraged for mushrooms. My son and his wife inspire me with their healthy lifestyle and diet. During our visit, Joe announced he was considering retiring from electrician work to focus on alternative building methods for energy-efficient housing. With his mad skills and creativity, and Gretchen's full support for the plan, my son is poised to follow his passion.

Threshold Choir practices took me north again with another night at the Dismal Ditch Rest Stop. This time the city lights across the channel appeared sporadically when the misty rain shroud lifted for a bit. The blanket of clouds that settled on the river was an invitation to dreamy sleep. The next day brought the gifts of sunshine and showers, and an explosion of October color in the trees as I followed Highway 30 east along the southern shoreline of the magnificent Columbia.

According to my friend, Sandor, Wanda's bank of three skylight windows give the van the appearance of a 1950s Saturday matinee spaceship. Those overhead windows were my ticket to a water globe afternoon at an autumn-flushed park on Sauvie Island near Portland. While eating lunch at my little table under the skylights, an upward blast of wind liberated golden leaves from all the trees at once, launching them high into the sky. The feather shaped leaves were suspended mid-air for a few moments until they slowly floated down from above, like snowflakes, landing on the glass above my head.

Counting Fish

Just thirty minutes from Portland lies another world: the Columbia River Gorge National Scenic Area. Its waterfalls, forest trails, and weathered rock formations draw locals and tourists alike. On this day, people foraging for mushrooms could be seen combing the woods with their baskets in hand.

At the Bonneville Dam, I went down to the basement where a window on the underwater fish-ladder makes it possible to view salmon and steelhead furiously swimming against the current in the concrete and steel maze. Fish counters track the numbers of each species making their way through the fish ladder each day. Chinook, sockeye, and coho salmon counts in 2019 were one-half to one-third the counts from fifteen years ago.

Because of catastrophic declines in salmon populations, on Indigenous People's Day (aka Columbus Day), 2019, inhabitants of the Columbia River Gorge made a public request to remove the dams on the Columbia. Without a free-flowing river, they fear the salmon they are charged to protect will disappear. Chinook salmon populations not only provide for the Native people of this region, their survival impacts the livelihood of members of northern tribes who hunt orca off the coasts of Washington, Canada, Alaska, and the Arctic. With fish numbers crashing, starving orca populations are in big trouble and are currently listed as endangered.

The Yakima Nation Chairman, JoDe Goudy, made this statement; "We have a choice, and it's one or the other: dams or salmon." To honor the ways of the ancestors, and to provide for the future generations of all creatures that depend on the species, Native people choose salmon. With 40,000 jobs and electricity production for the entire northwest hanging in the balance, the salmon and the tribes that seek their protection are likely to continue to lose this fight.

The Columbia Gorge Threshold Singers were focused on learning repertoire when I joined the new chapter at a church in downtown Hood River. Marty Mariette's lovely "Pure Grace," was one of the songs we worked on together.

After the practice, the chapter's director, Kalama, offered her driveway for an overnight in White Salmon, on the Washington side of the river. I followed her across the Columbia on an impossibly narrow truss bridge with wimpy six-inch guardrails that looked to be made of tinfoil. It may be less frightening to traverse the hundred-year-old bridge in the daylight, when the river below is not a black abyss, but I didn't test this theory. Avoiding a repeat of that white-knuckle crossing, I drove miles out of my way to find more substantial bridges during my exploration of the Washington and Oregon sides of the gorge.

When it was time to leave, river songs surfaced as I followed the water flowing back toward the sea. "The Healing Water," by Penelope Salinger, was one of the songs that bubbled up from that knowing place within.

CHAPTER 18

All Who Wander Are Not Lost

Vicki and Murray have created a symphony of color in their Corvallis home, where walls of amethyst, emerald, jade, and coral meet a plush sea of vibrant aquamarine carpeting. Legally blind, Vicki delights in the colors that manage to penetrate her vision and brighten her days. She told me she felt color-starved after two years living within the white walls of an apartment in Monterey, where we met singing with Lisa G. Littlebird's community chorus. An exceptional singer, songwriter, author, humorist, motivational speaker, and personal coach, Vicki recently added professional storyteller to her long list of skills.

Our visits are feasts of food, drink, songs, and politics. This time around, we discussed the elements of a good story. Her feedback was encouraging and helpful in my quest to gather momentum for my book project. Her take-home message: don't waste the listener's (or reader's) time with unnecessary words. Good reader, even when I don't hit the mark, please know I seek to honor you in this way.

After three days of recharging at Vicki's, the coast called me back again, but this time, finding overnight camping would be more challenging. Since my last visit, the authorities have responded to the growing popularity of RV travel by posting *Day Use Only* signs at pullouts and rest stops. My overnight options in Oregon would be limited to driveways, noisy rest stops inland along Interstate 5, or campgrounds with steep nightly fees. At the

Beachside State Campground south of Waldport, hard rain and pounding surf kept me on high alert after reading the sign at the campground entrance, "*Caution, high surf and heavy rain can flood the campground.*" During a break in the rain, I tried walking the beach, but wind-whipped sand sent me back to the protection of my van. The hundreds of miles of Oregon coastline offer picturesque beaches, but precious few days of beach weather.

Taking refuge from the wind and rain in the tiny Waldport Public Library, I was focused on my computer when I heard the tapping of a cane as a group of three moved toward a tall bookshelf behind me. It took me a moment to realize that the frail-looking elder with a voice as thin as her tiny bent body was a librarian, competently leading a couple to the book they sought. I felt compelled to watch as she worked the room in a worn, knee-length cotton dress that exposed impossibly slender legs marked with the blood bruises that bloom on aged skin. The regulars at this library knew the seasoned employee and, unlike me, they exhibited no surprise at her resolve. This remarkable elder is proof that advanced age doesn't have to stop us from doing what we are called to do.

Arranging to spend a night at an enchanted private property on the Alsea River required two full days of gate key coordination with Ellie, another friend from Wholehearted Chorus, who was in Switzerland and nine hours ahead in time, and her sister, Jinny, who lives in Portland. The limited phone service that is standard fare on the coast of Oregon didn't help with communication.

Grey skies and soft, intermittent rain cast a *Mists of Avalon* quality over lush "Riverhaven" on the afternoon I arrived. Weathered art objects peeking from the dense foliage add to the magic of the place that was once the home of Ellie's grandparents. Fallen leaves in mottled hues of gold, green, and brown, some more than twelve inches across, covered the ground with an earthy tapestry.

A glimpse of blue hydrangea flowers among the ferns and blackberry vines hinted that Ellie's grandmother once tended a formal flower garden on the riverbank. Closer inspection revealed that chameleon-like hydrangea blossoms as large as basketballs had taken over this secret garden, adopting the green colors around them to blend in with the surroundings.

From the Kincade family's sanctuary, I drove back to the coast on a winding mountain road with a continuous stream of golden leaves raining down and plastering themselves on the windshield like open hands.

The estuary where the river meets Alsea Bay was the perfect place for my morning coffee ritual. Boiling the water, assembling the coffee filter and cup, measuring the grounds, pouring a small amount of hot water, waiting a few moments for the grounds to swell, and adding more water, a little at a time: my morning coffee habit feeds more more than physical dependency. The predictability of this zen-like task is comforting. Familiar routines take on greater significance when each day presents such a wealth of new experiences. I found it important to lean into ritual and ceremony to mark the passage of time, and to remind myself to pause and step off the treadmill of forward motion.

In the Company of Travelers

Many years ago, my friend, Candace, told me about her journey to Japan to study with an acupuncturist of great renown. With no invitation or introduction, she showed up at his door. When the surprised acupuncturist asked who she was, she answered, "A traveler." That humble declaration won her an apprenticeship. Many consider traveling an honorable calling. A week wandering with no commitments provided an opening for connecting with other travelers drawn to the glories of the Oregon coast in the off-season.

During another visit to the Waldport Library, a large man sporting a long, remarkably dense white beard that lifted and fell as he spoke, held staff captive behind the library counter. In a booming voice that could not be ignored, he regaled them with details about his life and losses. Hearing him talk about living in his van, I asked if he knew of any free overnight parking in the area.

In the conversation that followed, Scott told me he stays in state campgrounds, where he pays discounted fees as a disabled Vietnam War veteran. He also explained his technique for juicing pomegranates while on the road, a daily routine that he credits for keeping him alive. This "Adventure Gypsy," as he calls himself, told me he has lived on the road for fifty years. With no taste for staying put, he spends winters in Arizona and summers on the Oregon and California coast in a custom-built camper van no bigger than mine. Scott's joyful spirit lit up the gray morning. We said good-bye with a shared chorus of "Happy Trails."

Another traveler was drying his belongings after a heavy rain shower on the morning we met at the Alsea Bay Historic Interpretive Center. Mike told me he had walked from Michigan to the coast of Oregon. When I mentioned Detroit was my birthplace, we discovered we were born in the same hospital, just months apart. Even more remarkable, this retired truck driver has leukemia and plans to keep walking until he can't.

The following day, I picked up a young woman hitch-hiking with a heavy backpack. Dawn was on her way to the Olympic Peninsula after a summer of traveling to workshops and interviews at alternative preschools in California and Oregon. With no job prospects on the horizon, she would pursue her dream of offering assistance to homeschoolers, and the parents of kids with autism and Down Syndrome in her own town.

She slept at Triangle Lake the previous night, where she managed to stay dry in the pouring rain by securing a tarp over her sleeping bag at just the right angle. She said all went well until she started out in the morning and was drenched by a downpour. It was around 5:00 p.m. when Dawn requested I drop her off along the highway. She hadn't the foggiest idea where she would sleep that night; catching sunset on the water was her only concern.

At picturesque Yaquina Bay State Park and Light-house at Newport Bay, I met Claudia, a docent volunteer. A full-time RVer for fourteen years, she told me she has volunteered or worked at parks around the country, but in recent years, she chooses not to leave the Oregon and Washington coast. She said it all started with a remote online job, and by the time the job ended, she was eligible for Social Security and hooked on the lifestyle. She gets by accepting park jobs that provide RV parking and utility hook-ups, and sometimes paid employment. She warned that it is getting harder to find those positions available to single persons when parks can get two workers for the price of one by hiring a couple.

Traveling the Oregon Coast.

On a rainy afternoon, I stopped for hot soup at the Pelican Brewery in Pacific City and met a friendly home-schooling mom carrying a motorcycle helmet. She told me about riding her motorcycle 100 miles from Portland in the rain that morning. This was her first motorcycle trip without her husband, and it was hard for her. She said that she challenges herself to do something "hard" every day, then journals about the challenges she tackles, and reviews her achievements each quarter before making plans for future challenges.

With a long-standing ritual of reviewing my own endeavors of the past year on New Year's Day, I know how empowering that exercise can be. For me, dedicating time to take stock of what has been accomplished, and of equal value, what was attempted, is a rewarding shift in focus that provides respite from the barrage of things that "need to be done."

Seduced by the Written Word

Nearing the one-year anniversary of my Threshold Choir tour, I felt the need to start organizing ideas for this book. The discipline of writing down my thoughts and experiences requires reaching backward into memory, notes, and blog posts to reassemble what has transpired. Although the blog helped me develop a daily writing routine, stepping out of the marvelous now to write about past events often meets resistance. Riding the river of words that flows when I'm in the zone is great, but convincing myself it's time to stop experiencing to write about my experiences does not come easily. I hoped that a night at the Sylvia Beach Hotel would be a kick-start for the book project.

In its latest incarnation, each of the twenty rooms in this century-old hotel is named for an author and decorated in a style befitting that author and their books. The beachfront hotel is named after Sylvia Beach, whose *Shakespeare and Company* bookstore in Paris is a literary landmark.

My Gertrude Stein room, with its faded rose chintz

bedspread and draperies, was modest in comparison to the rooms designed to honor Amy Tan, Agatha Christie, and F. Scott Fitzgerald, but it was comfortable in its shabby chicness.

Looking to this literary haven for the spark I needed to begin the monumental undertaking that a book project represents, I found myself giving in to the temptation of the cozy attic library instead. I passed an idyllic afternoon curled up in a worn overstuffed chair with a glass of champagne and a stack of books at my side, reading, not writing. Exploring the eclectic collection of shelved books, I grabbed whatever caught my attention, trusting that randomly opening the chosen book would reveal the nuggets of wisdom and beauty I sought in that moment. With sun streaming through the French doors and an expansive view of the beach and endless rows of glistening waves below, I waded through books in the attic until it was time to meet my son, who drove down from Lincoln City to take me to dinner.

The Central Oregon Coast is a hot spot for the arts, and following my night at the hotel, I walked next door to the Newport Performing Arts Center for a Saturday performance of Jules Massenet's opera, *Manon*, streamed from New York's Metropolitan Opera House. The soul-penetrating voices, elaborate costumes, and drama of opera never fail to thrill me, and though far from the Met, I managed to view many seasons of live-streamed performances at movie theaters in Monterey. The close-ups, interviews with performers, and backstage view of set changes add to the excitement of the live telecasts. Enamored by the idea of dressing up for the opera, even with a limited traveling wardrobe, I gave it my best shot. I unpacked my tall boots and my shin-length sweater adorned with autumn leaves to attend the show.

Even with days of clear skies, white sand beaches, and sunlight glimmering on the surface of the sea, the hustle to find overnight parking at the coast was wearing on me. It was time to move on. Having maxed out my budgeted campground limit for the month with more than a week before my next choir practice in southern Oregon, I reached out to old friends who had moved from Glen Ellen to Portland. An enthusiastic invitation from the Crawfords sent me north again, hundreds of miles in the opposite direction of my next choir stop.

From Macabre to Sacred

A dozen years had passed since I had seen the cultured friends who would graciously introduce me to the sights of their Portland. We rode the downtown aerial tram, ate at bohemian restaurants, attended a writing class, and visited the Chinese Garden and art museums.

Sky, their oldest son, lives nearby with his wife and two kids, and we spent Halloween reveling in his kid-centric neighborhood. Sky and his neighbors go all out for this holiday with ghastly decorations and elaborate costumes. A Las Vegas-style Elvis impersonator hired to perform in a front yard each year draws hundreds of costumed adult fans. It is a party on such a grand scale that residents have to stockpile enough candy to hand out to at least 1,000 trick-or-treaters each year. We took turns staffing the candy distribution at Sky's house, charged with the monumental responsibility of limiting the take to one piece of candy per child to insure the supply would make it to the end of the night. When Sky and Amy purchased the house, they were required to sign a disclosure warning them of the Halloween crowds.

Shifting from the macabre dynamic of Halloween to a friendly welcome extended to the spirits of the dead, we celebrated Día de los Muertos with a story circle. We decorated the Crawford's living room, hanging "papel picado," the cut paper banners that allow spirits to pass between the worlds, and created a tabletop altar with *offerendas* and flowers, fall foliage, candles, and photos.

Among the stories shared that night, Sky's experience on a surfing expedition near Shelter Cove on the Lost Coast of California gave me goosebumps. He told of camping alone in a ravine deep in the woods where the Mattole tribe and other Native people spent part of the year in fishing camps before their forced relocation to reservations in 1856. With no one for miles around, Sky heard native drumming floating on the still night air, and told of his astonishment seeing the drumming ignite his thoroughly extinguished campfire.

A Humble Gift

From the onset of the journey, I carried two cans of smoked oysters. I don't like canned oysters, but I kept them onboard as emergency rations. The tins were in the way the entire trip and no matter where I stashed them, they frequently fell out when I opened the pantry. Months before, I had decided to hand them over to the next hungry-looking person I saw, but the opportunity to give them away did not present itself until I stopped at a rest stop somewhere between Portland and Medford. A woman holding a baby and a sign asking for help was a candidate more than worthy of the offering. Actually, I never did see or hear a baby, I can only assume that within the bundled blanket nestled in the crook of her arm there was a sleeping infant.

Approaching the mom, or mom poser as she may have been, I explained that I couldn't help financially, but I would like to give her oysters packed in olive oil. I immediately regretted mentioning the olive oil, as if oysters packed in a lesser liquid might not be as grand a gift. My meager donation was graciously accepted.

Southern Oregon was ablaze in fall colors when I arrived in Medford. It was great to see Amrita, who was a member of the Aromas Threshold Choir chapter that tutored me when I joined TCI. Living in the hills above Medford with her husband, Dennis, their panoramic view of a patchwork of pear orchards is undergoing radical change as the popularity of CBD oil motivates local farmers to tear out orchards to plant profitable hemp. The hemp farms near Amrita utilize overhead chemical spraying and cover the soil around the plants with acres of plastic, similar to the toxic methods of production used by California strawberry growers. Only organic hemp is grown sustainably.

Like Amrita, many of the members participating in the Southern Oregon Threshold Choir practice I attended have nearly two decades of experience singing at bedsides. Their sound is infused with heavenly harmonies. Weeks had passed since my last chapter visit and I was looking forward to time with my friend, and eager to join this accomplished choir singing songs of the heart. We ended the practice with "So Many Angels," which perfectly describes the feeling of being surrounded by angels that comes over me in a circle of Threshold Choir singers.

With the California border not far from Medford, I left Oregon twelve months after starting my choir tour in Corvallis. I had budgeted for a year on the road, but I wasn't ready to end the adventure. In truth, with no home to return to, I didn't know how to end it.

Crossing into California, there was tension in the air. The two-legged, four-legged, and no-legged inhabitants of this place were all on high alert for fire. I camped on a southern slope of 10,000-foot high Mt. Shasta, in the midst of a sparse forest of pines and fir trees with a smattering of oaks, manzanita, and dry grasses. This parched land is cursed with thin rocky soil that doesn't retain moisture. The wide swaths of fire-blackened trees sparked a memory. In grade school, we learned that the twisted, wine-colored branches of manzanita are fire re-sistant, and the seeds need fire to germinate. That may explain why fire-prone California is the first place I have countered manzanita on this journey.

CHAPTER 19

Songbaths

The camp host gig I had arranged for wintering in Big Sur would not be mine until the Park Service received the results of a California Live Scan background check, and the ranger was concerned about getting the results well before my start date in January. Coming from Oregon, Redding was the closest city where I could get the fingerprinting done, the last hurdle to completing my camp host job application. Once that task was completed, I made arrangements to meet a friend for dinner.

Another California community traumatized by fire, Redding was ravaged by the Carr Fire that started in August of 2018 and raged for months, taking eight lives and burning 230,000 acres. Keith's was one of 1,100 homes lost to the inferno. The loss and subsequent interactions with the insurance company have been crushing for him. When last we spoke, he was dealing with the heartbreak and expense of removing fire-ravaged oaks from his property, trees that didn't come back to life with the winter rains as he had hoped. At dinner, he told me of his dream to leave the fiasco behind to bicycle to South America.

Traveling south just far enough to catch Highway 20 west, I crossed the coastal mountains to Mendocino with windows wide open to the refreshing "coming home smell" of the redwood forest. The coast was shrouded in cool fog when I arrived. After a couple of nights camping at the State Park in Mendocino, with no commitments, I stretched the four-hour drive to Sonoma to six days.

Salt Point State Park provided a campsite with un-obstructed views of the turbulent Pacific. Remarkably, with all the time I have spent wandering the Sonoma Coast over the past three decades, I had not stopped here before. In Gerstle Cove, the discovery of *Tofoni* held me spellbound. It is hard to believe that the weird and wonderful patterns of salt spray hardened stone that appear to creep over the pale sandstone in a dark web of honeycomb cells is not alive. I spent days studying the unique art of sea, salt, and time-etched stone that embellishes this coastline.

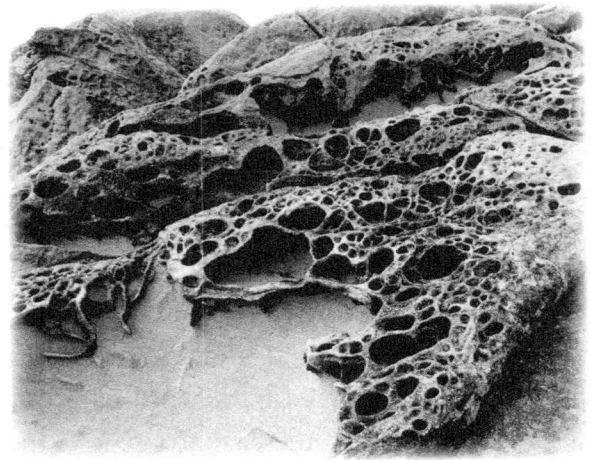

Fascinated by Tofoni.

Farther south, I could not pass the estuary at Jenner without stopping at the Russian River. I know this river well after many years swimming and kayaking in its warm water, taking fifth graders to the hatchery to collect eggs for raising steelhead in their classrooms, watching osprey carry humongous branches to treetop nests on its shores, and celebrating the river at the annual Russian River Festival.

That sacred ceremony held where the river meets the sea always closed with a blessing, a very long prayer given by a Coast Miwok elder in the language of the Native people of the region. One year, Tibetan monks in scarlet robes and yellow headdresses poured colored sand into the sea from a mandala they had created to raise awareness of the repression taking place in Tibet. They chanted and played tinny horns as part of the closing ceremony. I still get emotional thinking about the year a dense fog rolled in and a bagpiper, barely visible in the low lying clouds, closed the festival playing "Skye Boat Song." On this sunny morning, I parked next to the water and prepared an exquisite chilaquiles brunch with a poached egg, avocado, tortilla chips, and salsa.

Continuing south on the Sonoma Coast, I walked the cliffs of Bodega Head for the first time in many years. My desire to be near the ocean compelled me to make the fifty-minute drive to Bodega Bay frequently during the years I lived in Glen Ellen. At the base of the headlands, the fenced 120-foot-deep pond is all that remains of the nuclear power plant that was under construction on this site when a campaign by environmental activists put a stop to it.

As a member of Earth Elders of Sonoma County, I had the privilege to meet Dr. Joel Hedgpeth, the wise science professor who came up with the plan to release helium balloons from the site to alert the media and the public to the danger of building a nuclear power plant within 200 feet of the San Andreas Fault. The 1,500 balloons released on Memorial Day, 1963, traveled one-hundred miles inland, revealing how far contamination would travel on the wind, if, or should I say, when, an earthquake occurs along California's most notorious fault line. A faded sign now identifies the location as "Hole in the Head."

Spectacular beach weather in Northern California drew me to a campground on the sand spit at the mouth of Bodega Bay. It was 2:00 p.m. on a Sunday afternoon, check-in time at Doran Campground, and the only time I was likely to find a vacancy. I secured a campsite with views of the ocean on one side and the bay on the other. It was pure joy to run barefoot in the sand and play in the cold water. I fell asleep to the sound of the gentle waves and a recording of Helen Greenspan's lullaby, "Ocean Breath" playing on my phone.

Phone reception at the campground allowed me to retrieve a message from friends and former neighbors, Ritch and Margie, graciously inviting me to park in their Glen Ellen driveway for as many days, weeks, or months as I needed. I am always humbled by their generosity.

With the Foster's driveway as my Sonoma County base camp, I made plans for the final choir stops of the pilgrimage. I visited Sudie at another Napa Valley Choir practice and sang with friends in the Valley of the Moon Threshold Choir again. It was my good fortune to be invited to participate in the songbath led by the Sonoma County Threshold Singers each month at the Kaiser Hospital in Santa Rosa.

The Sound of Kindness

The November 2019 songbath offering at Kaiser drew twenty singers from the Valley of the Moon chapter and the Sonoma County Threshold Singers. In a meeting room at the facility, we arranged chairs in a large circle around two reclining lounge chairs while two choir members walked the halls of the hospital extending invitations to care providers, patients, and visiting family. After a vocal warm-up, a small group of choir members left the room to sing at patients' bedsides while the rest of us took our places in the circle, with some seated on stools close to the reclining chairs in the center of the room.

As those coming to receive singing slowly streamed into the room and took seats, Venus, the director of the Sonoma County chapter, led us in heavenly harmonies. The songs and the silence held between songs trans-formed the austere fluorescent-lit conference room into a sacred sanctuary. After receiving three or four songs in the reclining chairs, visitors familiar with the process made room for the next recipient by moving to the larger circle, or, in the case of medical staff, returning to their duties. We sang to patients, family members, nurses, and a former patient who comes back for the comfort of the singing each month.

Offering monthly songbaths to the public may have started with the Santa Cruz Threshold Singers in 2012. With the pandemic, the chapter expanded their reach by shifting the monthly offering to Zoom. Susan Moren was a recipient of in-person songbaths in Santa Cruz. She said this about the first time she was sung to in the chair, "It is a deeply personal experience to be sung to rather than sung for. It sounded like a chorus of angels around me. I felt I could die now, willing to be taken away. The ease and the blend is the key that opens the door."

Threshold Choirs around the world offer songbaths in their communities. Our chapter was inspired to start monthly songbaths in 2016. We put notices in the local newspaper inviting neighbors to experience the gift of being bathed in song. It felt like a revolutionary act of kindness to invite strangers to the living room where we practiced, make them comfortable in the reclining chair, offer to cover them with a cozy blanket, and softly sing over them for twenty minutes. The intimate setting drew people suffering physical and mental unease who were not comfortable inviting us to their homes to sing.

According to Kate, Threshold Choirs began offering song and songbaths to the public when troubling times created a "need for this service in our communities." Marti, the director of the Santa Cruz Threshold Singers, told of being asked if they could do something after the murder of a young girl in 2015 left that community in shock. The choir brought reclining chairs to a local community center to sing to those who came seeking comfort.

In that same year, a tragic shooting killed nine members of the Emanuel African Methodist Episcopal Church in Charleston. People were devastated by the horror of the hate crime, and touched by the forgiveness offered by members of the congregation. Pat Keown, director of the Threshold Choir of the Low Country in South Carolina wanted to offer support. "Singing was what we could offer; it was a way to pay our respects." The choir traveled to Charleston to sing outside the church and returned to sing on the streets of Charleston when the community came together for a service for the victims and their families. Pat told me, "You never forget that you were there."

Response to the Sonoma County Fires

Songbaths were offered to comfort evacuees following the Tubbs fire that ravaged Northern California in 2017. One of 68,000 residents forced to evacuate their homes, Venus Maher said she felt "a desire to do something to give comfort." The first time she sang for evacuees in the shelters, no one was available to join her, so she sang alone. Not knowing if her own home had burned in those initial days of the firestorms, she was living with the same uncertainty as the shelter occupants. For Venus, singing in the shelters was a reminder that, "We are no different. This is us. Everyone is in this together."

In the days that followed, she led Threshold Choir members from Santa Rosa and Sonoma singing at the Santa Rosa Fairgrounds and Veterans Hall, and at the Petaluma Community Center, where they encountered rooms with as many as 400 to 500 evacuees, mostly strangers, sleeping on cots crammed tightly together. "Feeling the music was creating heart-to-heart connections, we sang for hours and didn't want to stop."

They sang quietly, moving from bed to bed, and also sang to large rooms filled with people. In Petaluma, they sometimes sang with musicians who also offered their services. Carefully considering which songs would be appropriate and supportive for the people they were singing to, they avoided words like "home" and "fire" that might be triggers for traumatized shelter occupants.

Venus told of singing to a pregnant woman a week

from her due date and singing "Happy Birthday" to a one-year-old. She said they encountered lots of children and families in the shelters, many of them Spanish speakers. "Singing in Spanish brought a huge response." Venus said she felt reassured seeing "a grandmother making lace doilies look up and smile when she heard the singing, and a teenaged boy asked, in Spanish, if I would like a hug." Some joined in when they sang the Mexican folk song, "De Colores." Venus recognized a regular bedside client, an elderly woman who has no teeth, mouthing the words to "My Grateful Heart."

Angela, a member of Valley of the Moon Threshold Choir, told of offering songs in Coffey Park with Venus on Christmas night, two months after the Tubbs fire took the lives of five residents and destroyed most of the homes in the subdivision. She described a spontaneous celebration in the ruins of the neighborhood with bands, generators, Christmas lights, food, and community coming together to celebrate life and renewal as they faced the daunting task of rebuilding.

Choir members returned to Sonoma County shelters bringing "song care" to thousands of residents who were evacuated for the Kincade fire in October of 2019. This was especially challenging for those who lost, or nearly lost, their homes two years earlier. Many evacuees in the shelter had rebuilt since the last fire and with the Kincade fire, they found themselves at risk of losing their homes a second time. Threshold Choir singers from Santa Rosa and Sonoma joined together to bring songs of support to comfort those housed in shelters during that difficult time.

Lulu's mother was one of the evacuees in both the 2017 fires and the Kincade fire in 2019. Living in a memory care facility in Santa Rosa, she was not doing well when Lulu last visited. Faraway in Northern Minnesota, the director of the Lovely Loons Threshold Choir made a call to Kate Munger when she could not get information about her mom's location and condition. She asked Kate if she knew of any choir members living near the Petaluma shelter, where she thought her mother would be. Kate volunteered her son, who lives in Petaluma, to check on Lulu's mom. Kalloch was quick to call her, search the shelter, and send a picture of her mom to let her know she was OK. Lulu told me she is deeply moved by the support she receives from the Threshold Choir family, and the many ways in which the choir enriches her life.

Serendipitous Treasure Boxes

Singing is not the only gift Threshold Choir members offered to the survivors of the Sonoma County fires. With her great wisdom and compassion, Kate Munger wasted no time sending requests to choir members worldwide asking for donations of meaningful personal treasures for those who lost everything in the 2017 fires.

When the boxes arrived, Kate coordinated with choir members to distribute the packages. Angela was with Kate, and other members of the Valley of the Moon chapter, when they gathered to sing and distribute the first eighteen treasure boxes in Sonoma. She told of the astonishing serendipity she witnessed as the contents of the sealed boxes were revealed.

One recipient was ecstatic when she opened a package containing a salt and pepper shaker set that matched the one that had once belonged to her grandmother and was used by her family every day before the fire. One woman received Waterford crystal glasses of the same pattern as the ones she'd lost in the fire. The one and only quilt sent in a treasure box was received by a family who had lost a beloved family heirloom quilt.

Angela was also present when families attended the second distribution of treasure boxes, and she spoke of similar serendipitous pairings that occurred. A husband and wife unwrapped one ceramic angel after another packed in the sealed box they selected. Through their tears, they explained that these angels would replace the angels they had collected over the years to remind them of the son they had lost. Another woman unwrapped time-weathered exotic masks and foreign art objects from her treasure box. This seemed like an odd gift to onlookers until they learned the woman had been a traveler whose collection of vintage masks and art objects from around the world had perished in the fire.

One of those treasure box recipients was present at the Kaiser Hospital songbath I attended. After receiving songs in one of the reclining chairs, a nurse with a stethoscope hanging from her neck recognized Angela as she looked around the circle expressing her gratitude to the singers. She explained that Angela had been present when she received a pearl necklace as a gift in one of the treasure boxes donated by Threshold Choir members after her Santa Rosa home and everything she owned was lost to fire in 2017. Forced to evacuate again with the October 2019

Kincade fire threatening her newly rebuilt home, she told us that the pearl necklace was one of the possessions she took with her, saying it is the oldest thing she owns now.

A Beautiful Finale

I drove to Davis, California, for the final chapter visit of this epic journey. Marion kindly hosted me and invited other chapter members for a potluck meal the evening I arrived. The warm welcome I received was touching, and seeing familiar faces from the gatherings we have attended together over the years reminds me that we are all part of something bigger. One choir, many voices.

At the practice the next day, I learned that members of the Davis Threshold Choir take turns leading the group. Allegra led the practice I attended, which she closed with a graceful interpretive dance while we sang together. Reaching out to each singer with sweeping arm movements, Allegra worked her way around the circle with her offering of love. The blissful faces of choir members celebrating song, service, and each other at that practice clearly express the deep connections that exist among members of this chapter, and within every one of the chapters I had the privilege to visit.

Davis Threshold Choir.

Epilogue

With Song as My Compass

My dream of touring Threshold Choirs and the country was realized thanks to fortunate timing and the kindness extended to me. I drove 33,000 miles, circumnavigated the US, and made three excursions into Canada to sing with sixty-two Threshold Choir chapters. I was also privileged to join community singing circles in Victoria, B.C., Florida, and Minnesota, and participated in singing retreats on the Central California coast and in New York State. Pinch me!

Traveling with all that I needed in terms of creature comforts, I was able to lose myself in the magnificence of deserts, mountains, forests, prairies, rivers, lakes, oceans, and the glories of the ever-changing sky. Of the 415 nights spent on the road, I camped 102 nights in choir members' driveways, and parked overnight on roadsides, at rest stops, campgrounds, farms, vineyards, and slept in parking lots at breweries, casinos, Walmarts, and at sixteen RV-friendly Cracker Barrel restaurants. I also spent precious time with friends and family along the way.

Luck traveled with me as I weathered fierce storms and dodged six tornadoes. There were no ordinary days. Because I traveled with no expectations, each day was a gem shining with new sights, insights, and adventure. The purpose that guided me on this journey led me to the love and support I needed to complete the mission.

Returning to Pacific Grove in December, 2019, even the unmatched beauty of Monterey Bay and the joy of reuniting with friends and community couldn't quell the unrest I felt. I was wobbly, a sailor trying to find land legs after a long sea voyage. I could no longer claim Pacific Grove as my home. In January, I moved to Pfeiffer Big Sur State Park to begin the camp host position that I had planned as a soft landing. I was fortunate to secure a campsite in a sheltering circle of redwoods alongside the Big Sur River where owls call in the night, the cries of red tail hawks pierce the afternoon calm, and the rush of winter rain gives voice to the river.

When the Coronavirus shelter-in-place order went into effect in March of 2020, the State Park was closed to campers. COVID-19 also put an abrupt halt to singing in groups and at bedsides. I lost my connection to the outside world when weekly singing with the Threshold Choir of Pacific Grove and the Big Sur Wholehearted Chorus were canceled. Invited to stay in the quiet sanctuary of the park until the end of April, writing became my focus as I hunkered down in the forest in my elfin pod. I was living in a world apart with minimal human contact, limited phone service, and no internet. I couldn't have dreamed up a more spectacular or secluded writer's retreat. The transition from constant movement to stillness gave my soul a chance to catch up.

Other than wintering in Big Sur, my only plan for life after the pilgrimage was to stay open to what the universe offers. It was my intention to sell the Roadtrek to restore funds to my shrunken savings account when the journey was over, but the pandemic changed that. Wanda offered a safe, affordable place to quarantine in the Monterey Bay area. I passed the long days of the spring, summer, and autumn of 2020 walking the beaches and watching the tides rise and fall while I wrote, read, napped, and prepared meals parked at the water's edge. After the sun set on the roiling sea each day, I spent the nights among the Monterey pines in a church parking lot, isolated, but safe, in my compact home.

Using my phone as a hotspot, I was able to tap into the interactive pandemic music scene online. Even with the Zoom sound delay that made it impossible to sing together, Threshold Choir, community songleaders, and professional musicians utilized the internet to connect with singing communities and share songs without the limitation of distance. The ability to continue to sing and interact with others via Zoom was a lifeline during those long months of shelter-in-place solitude.

With COVID-19 deaths spiraling upwards at an alarming rate, my own respiratory issues and age moved me to update my final exit plans. I prepared for the possibility of death by coronavirus by updating my health care directive, financial information, and contact list, and planning a beach bonfire Celebration of Life and ash-scattering ceremony. "Trees Grow Slow," "When Soul Meets Winter," "Holy Angels," and "My Grateful Heart" were songs I added to my exit song list. Reaching out to Threshold Choir members, friends, and family I asked if they would officiate a Zoom option for the memorial, if it was necessary. Addressing the fear generated by the pandemic helped me turn my attention back to the present.

After twenty-seven months of van living, a COVID safe part-time job opportunity provided the income I needed to rent a small place in Monterey. Despite my joy having a full kitchen, an oven, and miles of countertop space, moving indoors was an adjustment. Accustomed to a view of the night sky from my bed, during the first few months in the cottage, I was called to sleep under the living room skylights where I could observe the stars and moon inching their way across the sky. Wonder Driven Wanda traveled back to the Pacific Northwest with new owners at the helm.

With the availability of COVID-19 vaccinations, the Threshold Choir of Pacific Grove shifted from Zoom practices to meeting in person again. We were working toward resuming bedside singing and public songbaths when the spread of new variants put those plans on hold. Weekly practices continue, masked and distanced, as we explore new ways to deliver the gift of gentle song and continue to prepare for a time when we can safely sing at bedsides again.

With my pilgrimage and book completed, I begin the next chapter of this journey called life guided by songs, stars, and dreams. Dedicating myself to my passion has empowered me to walk away from aspects of my life that no longer serve me. Humbled by necessity, I am better at asking for and receiving help when necessary. I arrive at this threshold fully appreciating the beauty of belonging and the value of balancing solitude, service, and community.

We each hear our own song. May your life be blessed with purpose that makes your heart sing.

Acknowledgments

Thank you to all of the Threshold Choir members and community singers who welcomed me to practices and bedside singing, opened their hearts in deep conversation, and shared their time, driveways, meals, showers, and homemade biscuits. To those who followed my travels on my blog, and those who made contributions to my gas fund, I thank you for supporting my dream. Stumbling along with little idea of where I was going, when I would arrive, or what to expect when I got there, I was consistently rewarded with acceptance and belonging. It is my sincere wish to carry forward the gifts of kindness I have received along the way.

I am deeply grateful to visionary Kate Munger for creating an opportunity for so many of us to find purpose singing in service, and for establishing the culture of caring that is the essence of Threshold Choir. I wish to thank Lisa G. Littlebird for spreading the joy of singing in community with such generosity, love, and talent, and to recognize the magic she weaves bringing singers, songwriters, and songleaders together in ever-widening circles. To Sage Marie Stanzler, "Sing your lips off, babies" Melanie DeMore, Lyndsey Scott, Laurence Cole, Maria Culberson, Jody Healy, Annie Garretson, and to all whose songs, stories, and wisdom I share in this book, my praise and sincere gratitude for your offerings.

Thank you to the songs that calm us, bring joy and laughter, speak to our grief and sorrow, help us remember where we come from, guide us moving forward, and connect us to those with whom we sing, and to all who have been touched by those songs throughout time. I want to express my gratitude for the songs of profound beauty and depth that bring tears and the awareness that we are all one. To the songwriters, song carriers, and songleaders who bring those heartfelt songs into the light, many thanks for sharing your passion and your gifts. Deepest gratitude also to those who have invited us to bring song offerings to their bedsides at their most tender and vulnerable moments.

I also want to thank the friends who offered their support through the long and arduous writing process. I am forever grateful for the time and talent Joan Linton and Cathy Baird contributed to editing this book offering, and for the help received from patient and witty Adina Reynolds early in the process. To Kel, and to Patricia Hamilton of Park Place Publications, thank you for the work you have done to birth this book.

Mapping the Journey

2018

2019

1/1	TS of the East Bay, Oakland, CA
1/7	San Francisco TC, San Francisco, CA
1/9	Peninsula TC, Palo Alto, CA
1/11	Aromas TC, Aromas, CA
1/17	Songleader Retreat, Carmel Valley, CA
2/1	Santa Barbara TS, Santa Barbara, CA
2/4	RiverSong TC, Riverside, CA
2/10	TS of San Antonio, San Antonio, TX
2/11	TS of San Antonio, San Antonio, TX
2/19	TC NOLA, New Orleans, LA
2/20	TC NOLA-Bedside Sing, New Orleans, LA
2/27	Tallahassee Area TS, Tallahassee, FL
2/28	Velma Fry Sing , Tallahassee, FL
3/19	Sarasota TC, Sarasota, FL
4/2	Heart of Georgia TS, Macon. GA
4/4	Long Bay TS, Myrtle Beach, NC
4/8	Asheville TC, Asheville, NC
4/15	Blue Ridge TC, Harrisonburg, VA
4/17	Charlottesville TS–Beside Sing, Charlottesville, VA
4/23	TS of Washington D.C., Washington D.C.
4/24	Philadelphia TS, Philadelphia, PA
4/27	S. Hudson Valley-Bedside Sing, Hudson Valley, NY
5/6	Northbay TS, Swampscott, MA
5/13	Providence TS, Providence, RI
5/15	TS of Indian Hill Music, Littleton, MA
5/28	TC Cleveland, Cleveland, OH
5/31	Yellow Springs–Bedside Sing, Yellow Springs, OH
6/1	TS of Yellow Springs, Yellow Springs, OH
6/4	TS of Ann Arbor, Ann Arbor, MI
6/6	London Ontario TC, London, Ontario, Canada
6/16	Omega Institute Singing Retreat, Rhinebeck, NY

6/28	Great Lakes Erie TC, Eerie, PA
7/2	Hospice of Northwest Ohio TC, Perrysburg, OH
7/8	Pandera Singing, Evanston, IL
7/9	TS of Wheaton, Wheaton, IL
7/14	TS of the Chippewa Valley, Eau Claire, WI
7/15	Menomonie TS, Menomonie, WI
7/20	Morningstar Singers, Minneapolis, MN
7/23	Lovely Loons TC, Grand Rapids, MN
7/24	Lovely Loons-Bedside Sing, Grand Rapids, MN
8/17	Sandpoint Threshold Singers, Sandpoint, ID
8/21	Butte Montana TC, Butte, MT
9/3	Nampa TS, Nampa, ID
9/10	Clallam County TC, Port Angeles, WA
9/24	Whidbey Bedside Singers, Whidbey Island, WA
9/25	Seattle TS, Seattle, WA
9/26	Evergreen TC, Kirkland, WA
10/8	Portland TS, Portland, OR
10/10	Columbia Gorge TS, Hood River, OR
11/3	Southern Oregon TS, Medford, OR
11/14	Napa Valley TC, Napa, CA
11/18	Valley of the Moon TC, Glen Ellen, CA
11/20	Sonoma County TC-Songbath, Santa Rosa, CA
11/24	Davis TC, Davis, CA

In addition to the chapters I had the privilege to sing with at practices and bedsides, I am grateful to the choir members who kindly met with me when I was passing through, even when there was no practice scheduled.

Songwriter Credits/Soundtrack

This partial list of the songs mentioned in this book is included to provide songwriter credits and a DIY soundtrack for the journey. I have included links for songs in the Threshold Choir repertoire when a public recording is available.

Breathe Easy, ©2003 by Sherrin Loyd
Threshold Choir Repertoire

Dear One, ©2008 by Penelope Salinger
https://www.youtube.com/watch?v=mzVYfZLXAvU

Deeply Loved (You Are Loved)
©2007 by Marilyn Power Scott
https://www.youtube.com/watch?v=mzVYfZLXAvU

Don't Give Up, ©2005 by Becky Reardon
https://www.youtube.com/watch?v=V7o3GMe-saQ

Flowing Free, ©2016 *by* Lauren Lane Powell
https://www.reverbnation.com/laurenlanepowell/songs

From My Heart to Yours, ©2004 by Maria Culberson
https://www.pressdemocrat.com/article/news/threshold-choir-sings-soothing-songs-for-the-terminally-ill/

Forget Your Perfect Offering, words by Leonard Cohen, music attribution unknown
https://thebirdsings.com/forget-your-perfect-offering/

Good News, © 2016 Coco Love Alcorn 2016 Coco Love Alcorn
https://www.youtube.com/watch?v=kupq5oycQYU

Hallelujah, ©2009 by Karisha Longaker and Sarah Nutting (MaMuse)
https://www.youtube.com/watch?v=f7KQ4_-kVyg

Here in California, ©1980 Another Sundown Publishing Co. by Kate Wolf

Holy Angels, ©2008 Sara Thomsen
https://www.youtube.com/watch?v=MddARnvjJGQ

I'm A Wild One Now, by Sage Marie Stanzler, written 2012, © 2019
https://singingalive.org/2016/10/20/im-a-wild-one-now/

I Wish That I Could Show You, ©2013 Barbara McAfee
https://www.youtube.com/watch?v=MWk6klJNnmc

Lift Every Voice and Sing, Public Domain, Words by James Weldon Johnson, music by J Rosamond Johnson https://www.youtube.com/
tch?v=HweqkrvI6Z0&list=RDcwWhu8tw4nU&index=2

Lullaby, by Chris Williamson, ©1990 Wolf Moon Records
https://www.youtube.com/watch?v=pczcwoQxG-U

May Only Love Surround You, ©2013 by Patricia Hallam Threshold Choir Repertoire

May Peace Be With You, ©2015 Annie Garretson
https://www.youtube.com/watch?v=ujLPSpj8MQ0

Metta Sutta, words from Buddhist text, music by Unknown, arranged by Kate Munger
https://www.youtube.com/watch?v=j1Ecr9w-fRM

Mojuba, Traditional Yoruba Song
https://www.youtube.com/watch?v=j1Ecr9w-fRM

My Grateful Heart, ©11/2004 by Laura Fannon
https://www.riseupandsing.org/songs/my-grateful-heart

Navajo Prayer, ©2004 by Jody Healy
https://jodyhealymusic.com/store

Ocean Breath, ©2009 by Helen Greenspan
https://www.youtube.com/watch?v=EV5LUrzvOCs

Lead With Love, ©2016 by Melanie DeMore
https://www.youtube.com/watch?v=9w22S8foSbk

Oh Morning, by Laurence Cole, Public Domain
https://www.laurencecole.com/album/oh-morning/

Owl Moon, ©1995 by Bruce O'Brian
https://www.youtube.com/watch?v=CcW2rpQxdmY

Power of Kindness, ©2018 MaMuse by Karisha Longaker
and Sarah Nutting
https://www.youtube.com/watch?v=pfsRSoeC8Lg

Pure Grace, ©2011 by Marti Mariette
https://www.riseupandsing.org/songs/pure-grace

Sending You Light, ©1993 by Melanie DeMore
https://www.youtube.com/watch?v=cIsZuoNFtXg

Singing for our Lives, ©2002 Calico Tracks Music by
Holly Near
https://www.youtube.com/watch?v=RwBwJ4W2IGs

So Many Angels, ©11/2008 by Kate Munger and Karen
Drucker
https://www.riseupandsing.org/songs/so-many-angels

Sweet, Sweet, Dreams, ©2013 by Lauren Lane Powell
https://www.youtube.com/c/LaurenLanePowell/videos

Standing Stone, by Melanie DeMore © 2011 MeMa Music
https://www.riseupandsing.org/songs/standing-stone

The Healing Water, by Penelope Salinger © 2012 https://
www.youtube.com/watch?v=JP_s2LCxi2Q

The Way Knows the Way, ©2019 by Lyndsey Scott
https://soundcloud.com/thebirdsings/the-way-knows-the-way-by-lyndsey-scott

Trees Grow Slow, Public Domain, by Laurence Cole
https://www.laurencecole.com/album/trees-grow-slow/

Walking Each Other Home, ©3/2013 by Kate Munger
(words by Ram Dass, with permission)
https://www.youtube.com/watch?v=kFM0zzSzpHU&list=
PLMp1pq0tDWy5n33X3T07PIpVimTU_pQZJ&index=29

We Call This Place into Peace, ©6/2003 by Kate Munger
Threshold Choir Repertoire

When Soul Meets Winter, ©2011 by Kristen Longmeier &
Kri Schaffer
Threshold Choir Repertoire

You Are Not Alone, ©2011 by Kate Munger
https://www.facebook.com/watch/?v=2746348305589793

Endnotes

1   Carly Loveling - http://singingheartharmonies.com
2   Kate Munger - Threshold Choir.org
3   Mitch Albom, *Tuesdays With Morrie: An Old Man, A Young Man and Life's Greatest Lesson* (Doubleday; 1997)
4   Mathew Brunwasser, PRI, The World, "In Turkey, Sufi music is used to decrease patient stress." April 27, 2012, https://www.pri.org/stories/2012-04-27/turkey-sufi-music-used-decrease-patient-stress
5   Tarja Pölkki, Anne Korhonen, "The Effectiveness of Music on Pain Among Preterm Infants in the Neonatal   Intensive Care Unit: A Systematic Review." National Library of Medicine, April 28, 2012, https://pubmed.ncbi.nlm.nih.gov/27820525/#affiliation-1
6   https//:www.frontiersin.org/articles/10.3389/fnhum.2015.00518/ful
7   Mitch Albom, *Tuesdays With Morrie: An Old Man, A Young Man and Life's Greatest Lesson* (Doubleday; 1997) 127
8   Raymond A, Moody, M.D., *Life After Life* (MBB, Inc. 1975, Bantam Books, a Division of Bantam Doubleday Dell Publishing Group, Inc. 1976)
9   Linda Bryce, *The Courage to Care, Being Fully Present with the Dying* © 2021 Linda Bryce (Capucia, LLC)
10 Lisa G Littlebird - https://thebirdsings.com
11 Dr. Barbara Mossberg - http://www.barbaramossberg.com/about/
12 Melanie DeMore – www.melaniedemore.com
13 Annie Garretson, http://www.anniegarretsonmusic.com/annies-music/#1475129262185-f5abdc45-eb44
14 Marilyn Power Scott - https://gesundheitpublishing.com/about/
15 Jack Kornfield, *Bringing Home the Dharma* (2013, Penguin Books, Shambala Imprint)

16 Alive Inside YouTube®.
https://www.youtube.com/watch?v=iVWh1sF9TFk

17 Robinson Jeffers, "Vulture" 1962. Source: *The Collected Poetry of Robinson Jeffers* (Stanford University Press, 1988) 8

18 Lauren Lane Powell - https://youtube.com/c/Lauren LanePowell

19 Laurence Cole – https://www.laurencecole.com

20 MaMuse - http://www.mamuse.org

21 Heater Houston - https://heatherhoustonmusic.com

22 Barbara McAfee - barbara@barbaramcafee.com

23 Debbie Nargi Brown - https://www.debbienargi-brown.com

24 Glen Phillips - https://www.glenphillips.com

25 Marilyn Power Scott - https://gesundheitpublishing.com/about/

26 Vernon Bush - https://www.facebook.com/Vernon-Bush-216976560252/

27 Chorus America Staff, "Chorus America's New Impact Study Reveals Lifelong Benefits of Choral Singing," July 18, 2019, https://www.chorusamerica.org/publications/blog/

28 John Blacking, *How Musical is Man?* (University of Washington Press; Reprint edition, 1974)

29 Brian Boyd, *On the Origin of Stories: Evolution, Cognition, and Fiction*, (Harvard University Press 11/15/2010)

30 Paddy Scannell, *Why do People Sing? On Voice*, (Cambridge: Polity Press, 2019) 112-117

31 Robin Wall Kimmerer, *Braiding Sweetgrass, Indigenous Wisdom, Scientific Knowledge, and the Teachings of Plants.* (Minneapolis: Milkweed Editions, 2013) 221-222

32 Craig Werner, *A Change is Gonna Come, Music Race & The Soul of America*, (The University of Michigan Press, 2006) 13

33 ibid.

34 https://www.npr.org/2013/08/28/216482943/the-inspiring-force-of-we-shall-overcome

35 https://www.nytimes.com/2008/02/10/arts/music/10ratli.html

36 Stacy Horn, *Imperfect Harmony, Finding Happiness Singing with Others*, (Chapel Hill: Algonquin Books of Chapel Hill, 2013) 2

37 Lyndsey Scott. https://www.facebook.com/webelongcommunityofsong/

38 Barbara McAfee, "How Oral Tradition Singing Helps Us Live & Work Better Together" Youtube filmed 2017

39 Mary Oliver, "Mindful." *Why I Wake Early* (Beacon Press, 2004) 58

40 Robinson Jeffers, "Hurt Hawks." ©1932 and renewed 1960 by Robinson Jeffers. Source: *The Collected Poetry of Robinson Jeffers* (Stanford University Press, 1988) 165

41 Velma Frye – https://www.facebook.com/velmafrymusic/

42 John O'Donohue, *Anam Cara*: A Book of Celtic Wisdom (Cliff Street Books, an imprint of HarperCollins Publishers, 1997)

43 Mathew Fox, *Original Blessing* (Jeremy P. Tarcher/Putnam 2000)

44 Kathy Leo, *On the Breath of Song, The Practice of Bedside Singing for the Dying* (© 2016 Kathy Leo)

45 Bjorn Vickhoff, Helge Malmgren, Rickard Astrom, Gunnar Nyberg, Seth-Reino Ekströ, Mathias Engwall, Johan Snygg, Michael Nilson, Rebecka Jörnsten, "Music Structure Determines Heart Rate Variability of Singers." Frontiers in Psychology, Auditory Cognitive Neuroscience, July 9, 2013, https://doi.org/10.3389/fpsyg.2013.00334

46 Peter Wohlleben, *The Hidden Life of Trees, What They Feel, How They Communicate...Discoveries from A Secret World* (Greystone Books; First English Language Edition, 2016)

47 Suzanne Simard, *Finding the Mother Tree, Discovering the Wisdom of the Forest (Knopf 2021)*

48 Andy Goldsworthy art, https://www.livingyourwildcreativity.com/art-gallery-1-mitchell-1